MAKE MERRY

IN STEP AND SONG

About the Author

Bronwen Forbes shares dances, songs, and plays in workshops at various Pagan and Wiccan festivals, Pride Days, and conferences across the country. For four years, Bronwen was dance captain for the Washington Revels, an organization dedicated to preserving and sharing historical seasonal folk songs, dances, and stories from around the world.

MAKE MERRY
IN STEP AND SONG

A SEASONAL TREASURY OF MUSIC,
MUMMER'S PLAYS & CELEBRATIONS
IN THE ENGLISH FOLK TRADITION

BRONWEN FORBES

Llewellyn Publications
Woodbury, Minnesota

First Edition
First Printing, 2009

Cover design by Gavin Dayton Duffy
Interior book design by Joanna Willis
Interior illustrations on pages 7, 9–11, 15–17, 23, 65–66, 79, 82, and 146 by Mickie Mueller; all others by Llewellyn art department except pages 71 and 72. Page 71: Image of Betley Window courtesy Milne Special Collections and Archives Department, University of New Hampshire Library, Durham, NH. Page 72: Image courtesy Vaughan Williams Memorial Library, London.

For group use, readers may photocopy music and song lyrics except for "May Day Carol" on pages 103–104.

Llewellyn is a registered trademark of Llewellyn Worldwide, Ltd.

Library of Congress Cataloging-in-Publication Data
Forbes, Bronwen, 1963–
  Make merry in step and song : a seasonal treasury of music, mummer's plays & celebrations in the English folk tradition / Bronwen Forbes. — 1st ed.
        p.   cm.
  Includes bibliographical references (p.   ).
  ISBN 978-0-7387-1500-1
  1. Folklore—Great Britain. 2. Folk dancing, English—United States. 3. Mumming plays—United States. 4. Great Britain—Social life and customs. 5. United States—Social life and customs. I. Title.
  GR141.F67 2008
  398.20941—dc22

                                                                        2008003533

Llewellyn Publications
A Division of Llewellyn Worldwide, Ltd.
2143 Wooddale Drive, Dept. 978-0-7387-1500-1
Woodbury, MN 55125-2989, U.S.A.
www.llewellyn.com

 Printed in the United States of America on recycled paper

To my husband, A.G., and my daughter, Rose,
for their unconditional love and support of me and all my dreams.

And to Herman.
This book would never have been finished if it weren't for you.
Rest in peace, Best Dog Ever.

CONTENTS

ILLUSTRATIONS

Maypole Dance

Abbots Bromley Horn Dance

SONGS AND DANCE TUNES

ACKNOWLEDGEMENTS

Many writers start their acknowledgements with a cliché such as "The creation of a book like this is not the effort of one person alone," because it's true. The following people were instrumental in helping me with this project, and I'm glad I have an opportunity to publicly thank them.

First and foremost, I am grateful to my editors, Elysia Gallo and Mindy Keskinen at Llewellyn, for their hard work on the final draft of this book. Pagans aren't too enamored of saints, as a rule, but if we ever come together and elect a patron saint of patience with first-time authors, Elysia gets my vote. And for patron saint of doing whatever is needed to make a book the best it can be, I nominate Mindy.

I also could not have done this without my husband, A.G., and my daughter, Rose, for keeping the home fires burning while I sat at the computer, for being willing to pose for photos, and for insisting that I take breaks and bask in their company for a while, and, most of all, for putting up with my weirdness and occasional bursts of self-doubt and grumpiness. I love you two. A.G. also read an earlier draft and contributed some very useful suggestions that made the final version much more historically accurate.

My mother gets a huge thank-you for sharing her maypole dance routine with me. She also deserves my thanks for advocating on behalf of myself and other women who wanted to learn and perform morris in my hometown. By 1986, we were dancing alongside the guys in the classroom and on the street. Without her efforts, it would have taken even longer. Way to go, Mom!

My father is responsible for the transcription and notation of every tune and song in this book. The effort he put into his half of this project was every bit as long and labor-intensive as mine. Truly, he deserves coauthor credit.

Double thanks to both my parents for raising me to appreciate the power and beauty of the English folk tradition.

Malcolm Taylor and Peta Webb of the Vaughan Williams Memorial Library in London tracked down the origin and legal availability of maypole pictures. I am grateful for their time. Nancy Mason, special collections librarian at the University of New Hampshire Library, deserves special thanks for finding the Betley Window picture I needed, and for tracking down my copies of the picture when it was lost in the reproduction department.

Dr. Anthony Barrand was very generous with his knowledge of English folk music and the copyright authorities in England. My thanks for all his time and patience on my behalf with this and many other projects.

Finally, I want to thank Dr. Christopher Stasheff and Dr. Jim Lee, two of my professors at Eastern New Mexico University (and the best mentors ever!), for general hand-holding and sound career advice.

INTRODUCTION

. . . TRACES OF ANCIENT MYSTERY . . .

In the hilly, untamed, windswept country of Yorkshire, they blacken their faces and lift interwoven swords at the winter solstice to bring back the sun. On the sea-cradled Gower Peninsula in Wales, they sing a song wishing their friends and neighbors wes hal *or good health; one verse determines the proper time to sing it based upon the position of the moon and the stars.*

Amidst the golden-brown stone cottages of the Cotswold Hills, they dance with bells and ribbons, sticks, and handkerchiefs to drive the spirits of winter away and to wake up the Earth. On the rocky coasts of Cornwall, festive processions on Beltane morning recall ancient war victories and ensure good luck and fertility in the coming year.

When the heather blooms on the hills of Scotland and Ireland, they celebrate true love within its fragrant embrace and light bonfires to keep the sun alive.

As hunting season approaches in the woodlands of Lichfield, they dance with thousand-year-old reindeer horns to invoke the prey they seek. On the wild moors of the Isle of Man, children carry lanterns made of intricately carved turnips as they go from door to door singing "Hop Tu Naa" every Samhain.

In every place and every season throughout England, they reenact folk plays and sing songs that keep the memory of mystical beings and places alive, traditions to teach their children about magic and ritual, fertility and harvest, life and death.

In a small college town in central Kentucky, even at the beginning of the twenty-first century, most of these traditions are still carefully preserved; they are taught to local schoolchildren and shared at winter folk festivals. Consequently, the seasonal dances, songs, and stories of Great Britain have, over the past seventy-five years, spread throughout the New World. I was truly blessed to grow up in this town. The ritual dances and folk songs that were woven into the fabric of my childhood, I believe, led me to seek out the Neo-Pagan path in my early twenties. The ideas, symbols, and lore contained in these two disciplines are, in many instances, identical.

"How," I am often asked, "did you, who was born and raised in a good Christian home, grow up and become Pagan?"

"How," I always reply, "could I have been raised with the personification of the Horned God literally dancing before my eyes, as men I've known all my life perform a thousand-year-old Horn Dance every year, and become anything else?"

Mention the words "ritual dance" to most modern American Pagans, and what springs to mind are the dances of the Middle East, Africa, and Native America. Sadly, most of us are unfamiliar with the rich Pagan English heritage that has survived, albeit in fragments, in the dances, songs, and folk plays of Great Britain. The sole exception to this, the maypole dance performed by many groups at Beltane, is more often an exercise in hopelessly tangled ribbons than in folk tradition.

Most of my fellow Pagans do not know that the material contained in this book even exists. It is and has been my very great honor to continue, with this book, the process of reintroducing American Pagans to their pre-Christian British folk customs.

I invite you to pick up a sword, tie on some bells, dress up like a horse, raise your voice in song, and spend a year in the English folk tradition with me.

Bronwen Forbes
Winter 2008

WINTER

The assembled crowd hushes in anticipation as a lone musician steps into the cleared space. Among the spectators, four odd characters—a Fool, a Man-Woman, a Horse, and an Old King—watch with keen interest as the ritual dance unfolds. Characters older than the dance itself, three of them are here to bear witness, and one will join in when the right moment comes. Eight other men stand in a single line just out of sight of the crowd. Their faces are blackened with burnt cork as disguise, and the tips of their swords rest comfortably against their right collarbones, waiting for the musician's summons.

When it comes, the men quickly step into the waiting space and form a small circle. The blades of their swords catch and reflect the light as they meet in the center of the circle, raised high above each dancer's head. The music changes, faster now, and the dancers clash their swords together, then link up into a ring formation, each clasping the hilt of his own sword in one hand, the tip of his neighbor's in the other.

Without breaking the circle, they weave in and around each other, ducking under arches made of swords as they change direction again and again. The crowd watches silently, waiting.

The dancers crowd together into a tight cluster. There is a flurry of hand movements, of sword tips passed over and under, then the knot is locked into place. The crowd bursts into cheers and applause as the lead dancer raises all eight swords, now woven into an eight-pointed sun-shaped star, high above his head. The others follow their leader single file as he proudly dances around the small circle, displaying their creation to the people.

It is time. The man dressed as the Old King calmly makes his way to the center of the circle. As the lead dancer lowers the star of steel swords, he carefully places the core of the star over the Old King's head and around his unprotected neck. The others reclaim their sword hilts, and as the music becomes even faster, they dance around the King. Suddenly the music stops as each man quickly and simultaneously draws his sword out of the knot. The Old King falls to the ground.

There is much accusation and counter-accusation. Who has killed the Old King? The dancers censure each other, the Horse, the swords, and finally the Fool. But the blame falls on no one.

The body lying on the ground never moves . . .

Did I just describe the ritual killing of a Sacred King hundreds of years ago? Or did I merely recall a longsword dance and mummer's play demonstration that I saw at an annual folk festival in Kentucky on New Year's Eve as recently as 1998?

Or could I—possibly—have done both?

Sword Dance as Sacrifice

The longsword dance is just one of many seasonal rites passed down by English folk over the centuries, each generation learning by watching, listening, and doing. Other such traditions include the mummer's plays—humorous folk plays depicting the cycle of death and rebirth—seasonally themed songs, and, of course, a rich dance tradition including morris dances, maypole dancing, country dances, and the Abbots Bromley Horn Dance. We will examine all of these in this book. Folklorists first observed and "collected" many of these rituals in England over a hundred years ago, and this book joins that modern tradition of preserving them and spreading them more widely.

The longsword dance continues to be very popular in Britain and the United States, and is frequently performed by groups of all ages. Folklorists and scholars have found dances similar to it associated with religious ceremonies in some Latin cultures and with craft guilds in Scandinavian countries. The concept of a group of linked dancers—a chain-dance—imbued with ritual significance is certainly nothing new. Such circular dances were depicted in Egyptian temple art circa 3400 BCE, although it is too great a stretch to draw a direct connection from there to the modern longsword dance.

The *Johnson Dictionary* (1755) defines morris as "a dance in which bells are jingled or staves or swords clashed." A folklorist writing in the late nineteenth century in the journal *Shropshire Folk-Lore* prints a document from 1652 in which mention is made of "a morrice-daunce . . . with six sword bearers, one of whom, Thomas Lee, was most abusive." We will return to morris dancing in the Spring section of this book.

The significance of longsword dancing as a pre-Christian rite is very clear: it is a remnant of a Celtic solar-worship system. Traditionally, the dance is done between Yule and Twelfth Night (January 6), when the sun is at its weakest. The circular pattern of the dance and the dramatic raising of the sun-shaped sword lock can easily be interpreted as a ritual to help the sun return. The enthusiastic reaction of even modern, non-Pagan audiences when the lock is raised at the climax of the dance supports this idea.

For today's Pagan, the longsword dance is a ritualized representation of the sacrifice of the Dying God or the Sacred King, as in the legends of Tammuz, Osiris, Balder, Lugh, and John Barleycorn, to name a few.

Ritual human sacrifice is a subject most people are uncomfortable with, especially twenty-first-century Pagans. Throughout history, so many indigenous peoples and religious minority groups (including Jews and Christians at various times) have so often been wrongly accused of sacrificing people, especially children, that as followers of pre-Christian and/or indigenous faiths we tend to avoid or deny the topic entirely.

This is perfectly understandable, but to not look honestly at our heritage and our past, even the bloody and unpleasant parts, is to not fully accept the cycle of potential within each one of us. As we will shortly see when the longsword dance is combined with the mummer's folk play, dying for the land, the King, or the people, is merely a midpoint in the story. It is the completion of the sacred cycle, the rebirth or renewal—in the form of a new baby, next year's crop, or the rejuvenated hero—that makes the death so very important and so very sacred.

Scholars know that the ancient peoples of what is now England and Scotland practiced ritual human sacrifice. Sometimes this was voluntary. A person chosen by lottery would be sent to deliver a message of need to the gods on the "other side" in times of great social crisis, such as the Roman invasion in the early fourth century. Sometimes, however, the sacrifice was involuntary. In times of drought or other agricultural disaster, criminals or prisoners of war might be thrown into pits filled with large wooden upright spikes and then immediately buried to "feed" the soil.

In addition, the Celts are known to have been headhunters. They believed that they could control an enemy's spirit—or gain his skill, knowledge, and bravery—if the enemy's head was saved after the slaying. Often, a slain enemy's head was carefully preserved in a war temple. Archaeological evidence has found that, after death, a clan war leader's head was often kept in a separate shrine in his tomb. It is no stretch to connect the longsword dance with beheading.

Unfortunately, no concrete historical or archaeological evidence exists to confirm that the Sacred King or his substitute was sacrificed every seven years or some multiple of seven years. Accounts to the contrary are merely wishful thinking on the part of certain credulous early folklorists. Religious historians speculate that *if* the sacrifice of the King was ever practiced, it would have been in Neolithic times.

However, there is a great deal of *folkloric* evidence to support the concept of the sacrifice of a Sacred King. The strongest piece of evidence is probably the longsword dance, especially when performed in the context of the mummer's play, the traditional folk play depicting death and rebirth. After all, if an act is being simulated—mock wedding, mock sacrifice, mock feast—there is an excellent chance it was once done for real, and the mock version is a later symbolic substitution for the once very real thing.

It is easy to imagine what would happen if those swords were razor-sharp, someone's head was placed in the center of the lock, and the swords were drawn . . . and no one person could be blamed for the death. The sacrifice was considered to be at the hands of the gods; to claim responsibility would take it from the realm of the sacred and turn it into simple, ugly murder. Hence the ritual of group denial and blaming the Fool, who in ancient times stood outside the law, and could not be prosecuted.

This is one reason longsword dancers traditionally disguise themselves in some way, usually by blackening their faces with burnt cork. The villagers were able to pretend that they did not recognize the individual dancers, which again made the ritual denial of blame or guilt possible.

The custom of ritual denial is, of course, not limited to the aftermath of a longsword dance. Blame passed around a circle of people can be found in the ballad "Who Killed Cock Robin?" ("I," said the sparrow, "with my little bow and arrow." Who saw him die? "I," said the fly, "with my little eye.") Some old Scandinavian folk tales, too, include the concept. Celtic scholar Alexei Kondratiev, who grew up in rural France in the mid-1900s, recalled that children in his neighborhood often played a game that asked "Who killed the old woman's goat?" and consisted of a mock tribunal to determine the responsible party. Each child acted the role of a different animal and, taking turns around the circle, denied any responsibility for killing the goat. When all the children had finished, they all performed a short song refrain with an accompanying dance.

For the longsword dancers, another reason for even a rudimentary disguise was that it helped emotionally transform them from the simple miners, laborers, and farm workers they were in everyday life to the mystical, magical, sacred figures they became in the longsword dance. Think of how you feel in jeans or your day-job clothes at the grocery store, and compare that to how you feel in ritual garb at a Pagan festival or in circle.

NOTE TO PAGAN GROUPS DOING THE LONGSWORD DANCE

I recommend that participants dress in comfortable jeans or sweatpants and sturdy shoes. Lovely flowing ritual robes with great big sleeves are not practical for this activity, as they could get tangled up in the swords. The same goes for ritual necklaces and bracelets and ceremonial crowns. Nor do I recommend ritual nudity for longsword dancing, as there are many essential parts of one's anatomy (male and female) that might not be comfortable near a fast-moving sword, or even a facsimile of one!

In all seriousness, though: while it is impossible to separate the longsword dance from its powerful image of human sacrifice, I am not in any way advocating this rite's use as an instrument of such! Remember, there can be as much power in *mimicry* magic as there is in the actual act—and without the karmic price.

Participants should ground and center themselves before they begin, and personally ground any excess energy afterwards (see appendix B, "Grounding and Centering").

Kirkby Malzeard Longsword Dance: Instructions

Several villages in northern England have their own longsword dances. Here is an abridged version of the one performed by the men of Kirkby Malzeard.

Materials and Preparation

CLOTHING

Comfortable jeans or sweatpants and sturdy shoes are advisable for this intricate dance. Flowing garments and jewelry could be hazardous. See the "Note to Pagan Groups" above for more on this subject.

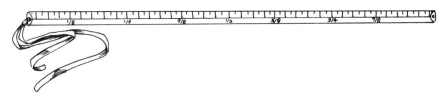

A wooden longsword from the Country Dance and Song Society of America and a yardstick with ribbon designating the handle.

SWORDS

Each dancer needs a sword, and all must be of identical length and thickness. Uniformity is key; if the sizes and styles vary, the interlocking sword star will fall apart!

In these dance instructions, *hilt* refers to the handle of the sword; *tip* or *point* refers to the other end, even though it may be blunt.

An affordable set of wooden dancing swords is available from the Country Dance and Song Society of America (see appendix A). Or you can make your own out of wooden slats, typically 1⅛ inches wide by a quarter-inch thick, found at most lumberyards. Cut the slats into three-foot lengths and sand them to prevent splinters. Shape a blunt point, if you wish. To simulate a hilt, paint, contour, or mark about four inches from one end. Mark them clearly: dancers will be holding both the hilt of their own swords and the point of their neighbor's sword. Household yardsticks also work as dancing swords, although they're less flexible. Many hardware stores and lumber companies give them away as free advertising. Simply paint over the markings. Most yardsticks have a hole in one end; you can tie a piece of brightly colored ribbon in it to designate the hilt.

Music

You will need music in 4/4 time with eight bars of primary melody ("A"), followed by eight bars of secondary melody ("B"). The traditional tune "Brighton Camp" works well, although it is not normally used for this dance. American folk music enthusiasts will recognize the melody as "The Girl I Left Behind Me."

Preliminaries

- You will need six to twelve dancers, all with identical swords. Six or eight is ideal. (With more than twelve, the interlocking sword star becomes unstable and might rain swords down on its carrier's head.)

- Number your dancers in a circle, counting off clockwise. Key positions for a six-person set are dancers 1, 5, and 6; for an eight-person set, dancers 1, 7, and 8. If they're not experienced folk dancers, they should at least be "spatially aware." Dancer 1 should be tallest and/or most experienced; this person gives verbal cues if needed, acts as the anchor during the clash figure, and lifts the sword lock overhead. The other two key dancers start the double-under figure, which takes reliable timing.

- All dancers: the hilt (handle) of your sword goes in your *right* hand. Leave it there!

- Other than some quiet cues from Dancer 1, the dancers should be silent. Let your demeanors reflect the tone of serious and somber ritual dance.

- Your sword hilt is in your *right* hand! (Just checking!)

The Step

The step is a loose yet energetic walking step. Walk—but look like you're dancing. Movement should be continuous, with no pauses between the dance figures.

Dance Instructions

OPENING SEQUENCE

1. *Circle with sword on right shoulder.* As the A music begins, dancers walk single file clockwise (left). Hold your sword in your right hand at hip level with its point on your own right shoulder. Keep circling until dancer 1 gives a signal. (Dancer 1: prepare to cue "clash!" as the B music begins.)

2. *The clash.* At the signal, all dancers keep circling, turn to the center, and raise swords in a teepee-pole formation. Dancer 1, hold your sword steady as an anchor to prevent tangling; all others clash swords by twisting the wrist rhythmically for 8 counts. (Dancer 1: prepare to cue "Link up!" if needed.)

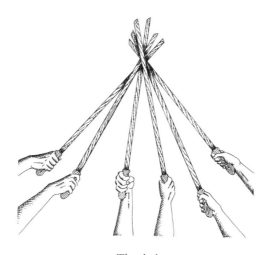

The clash.

3. *Link up.* All dancers: as you turn back into single file, carefully lower your sword point onto your own *left* shoulder and slide it slightly back and down toward the person behind you. (Keep the tip low, to avoid ritually sacrificing that person's eye.) Your right thumb is aimed at your throat, so try not to strangle yourself. As your front neighbor's sword point appears, grab it with your *left* hand, palm up, and keep circling. When everyone is linked, circle for another 8 counts. (Dancer 1: prepare to cue "Hilt to the right" if needed.)

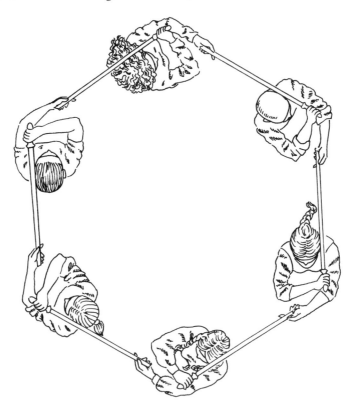

Linking up: Swords rest on the outside (left) shoulder.

4. *Hilt onto right shoulder.* Still circling, all dancers lift your hilt over your head and rest it on your own *right* shoulder. Keep holding your neighbor's sword tip with your left hand, adjusting spacing as needed. Circle for another 8 counts. (Dancer 1, prepare to cue "Hilt-and-point ring" if needed.)

Hilts now rest on the inside (right) shoulder.

5. *Hilt-and-point ring.* Still circling, all dancers open out into a large ring: slowly lift your hilt off your right shoulder, face in, and drop both hands to waist level. (Your right hand still holds your own hilt; your left hand still holds the tip of your neighbor's.) Be ready to start the double-under figure instantly when cued by dancer 1. The goal here is constant movement.

DOUBLE-UNDER FIGURE

In this figure, the circle almost turns inside out, then turns back again through a casting-off pattern. The figure is repeated as many times as there are dancers (six times for a six-person set). Don't let go of your sword, or your neighbor's! The hilt-and-point ring stays intact through the whole figure. And keep the formation tight; avoid wandering.

6. *Two dancers form an arch.* These options are for six or eight dancers.

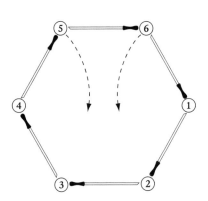

A. Dancers 5 and 6 move toward the center of the circle.

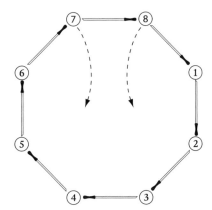

A. Dancers 7 and 8 move toward the center of the circle.

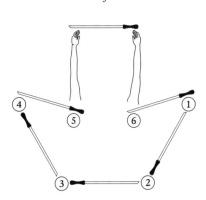

B. They raise 6's sword overhead to form an arch and step into the center, facing dancers 2 and 3.

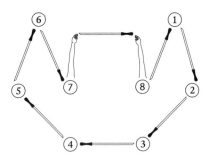

B. They raise 8's sword overhead to form an arch and step into the center, facing dancers 3 and 4.

7. *Pass under.* The other dancers pass under the arch. The first pair through the arch immediately forms a new arch using the sword between them (see below). The rest of the dancers follow, with the original archmakers dropping their arch.

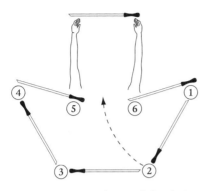

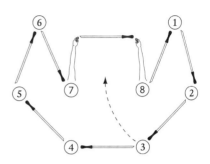

A. Dancers 2 and 3 step behind 2's sword and move under the arch, pulling other dancers with them.

B . Dancers 3 and 4 step behind 3's sword and move under the arch, pulling other dancers with them.

A second arch has been raised (and dancers are briefly positioned in reverse order from the original circle). Do not pause here; move directly to step 8.

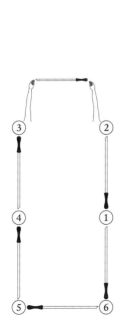

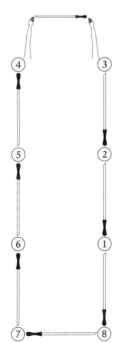

8. *Cast off to restore the original circle.* Staying linked, the new archmakers "peel off," walking the arch along to encompass the other dancers as described below. Tip for all dancers: hold your sword firmly but keep your arms and shoulders loose: "pretzel arms." Again, keep the formation tight; dancers should avoid drifting apart.

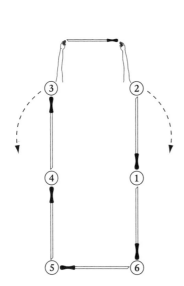

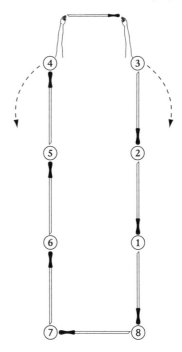

A. With sword still held high, the new archmakers (dancers 2 and 3) turn away from each other in place, making a full turn to face each other again. Holding the sword high and stretching to make room, they step sideways toward their starting positions, moving their arch over the other dancers' heads. All follow, ducking if necessary. Dancers are "unwinding" back to original order.

B. With sword still held high, the new archmakers (dancers 3 and 4) turn away from each other in place, making a full turn to face each other again. Holding the sword high and stretching to make room, they step sideways toward their starting positions, moving their arch over the other dancers' heads. All follow, ducking if necessary. Dancers are "unwinding" back to original order.

9. *Open out into the original circle.* As the circle falls back into place, the last dancers will do an underarm turn in place to fully unkink and restore the original hilt-and-point ring.

10. *Repeat the double-under figure with new archmakers.* Repeat steps 6 through 9 with different pairs of archmakers, until all neighboring pairs have done so.

    Six-person set: Next time, dancers 6 and 1 make the first arch, using dancer 6's sword. All pass through it, and the first ones through (dancers 3 and 4) make the second arch to reverse the circle. Continue all the way around the ring, starting with a different pair each time, for as many times as there are dancers.

    Eight-person set: Next time, dancers 8 and 1 make the first arch, using dancer 8's sword. All pass through it, and the first ones through (dancers 4 and 5) make the second arch to reverse the circle. Continue all the way around the ring, starting with a different pair each time, for as many times as there are dancers.

THE LOCK

11. *Repeat the opening sequence.* Repeat steps 1 through 5, ending circling left in the hilt-and-point ring. (Dancer 1, cue "Lock!" if needed.)

12. *Start the lock.* To begin interweaving all sword blades into a star: All face center and, keeping palms up, cross your *right* hand (holding hilt) OVER your *left* hand (holding point). Pass the point in your *left* hand to the person on your *right*. (In a moment, that sword will be passing in front of you without your hand on it.)

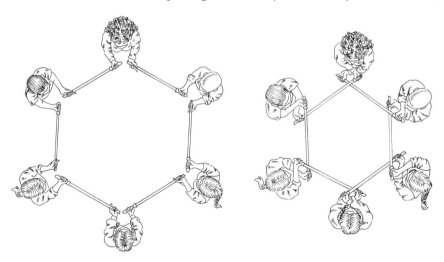

Start to make the lock. For an eight-person set, the technique is exactly the same.   *Right hand (hilt) over left hand (point).*

13. *Complete the lock.* All simultaneously: still keeping palms up, grasp the point coming toward you in your *left* hand and lock it in place OVER the hilt in your *right* hand. Look down at your blade. Starting from the hilt, it should be tucked under, over, under, then over, forming one side of the star. (Tip: Stand still while learning to make the lock, then practice doing it while circling.)

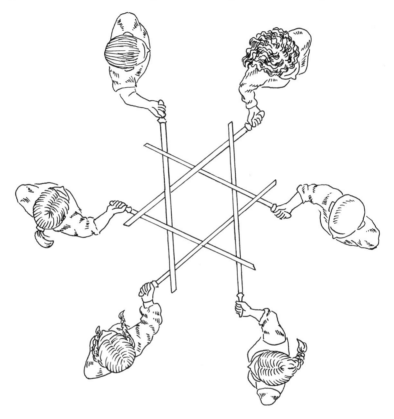

The completed lock.

14. *Lift the lock.* Dancer 1: Lift the star-shaped lock above your head and lead the other dancers single file in a circle, clockwise, looking admiringly at your creation. If you are planning to "behead" someone, now is the time for that person to come into the center of your circle.

15. *Release the lock.* Dancer 1: Lower the lock and hold it flat at the center of the circle. (For "beheading," gently place it over the head and neck of the sacrificial

Six-sword lock.   *Eight-sword lock.*

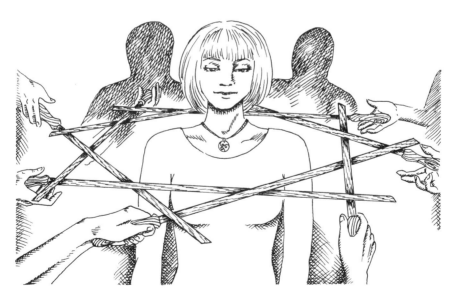

Lock with sacrificial victim all ready to "go."

person). All dancers grab a hilt in your *right* hand, circling single file. With your *left* hand, grab the *left* shoulder of your front neighbor. Circle once holding the lock at about shoulder height, counting to 8 in time with the music. On the count of 8 and not before, *quickly pull your sword out of the lock, straight and level.*

16. The dance is finished. Ground the excess energy.

The Mummer's Play: Story of Death and Rebirth

Even when performed by itself, the longsword dance is a very powerful ritual. But it is also done within the context of a simple play, and it is there we find its true meaning.

"Mummer's play" is an all-encompassing term for the various folk plays, telling of death and rebirth, that have been found throughout the British Isles. The oldest written reference to a mummer's play dates from December 1560: a note to pay "George, Mr. Pellam's man, to furnish himmselfe lord of Chrismas and him men in a lyvery 40s." It is unknown for how many centuries these plays existed as oral tradition; the oldest surviving intact text is commonly referred to as the Revesby Play, a handwritten script dated 1779. Many of the plays that were collected a hundred years ago or so bear a strong structural and textual resemblance to the mystery and morality plays that illustrated biblical stories to medieval churchgoers.

Remember the Fool, the Man-Woman, the Horse, and the Old King who were watching the longsword dance in the introduction to this section? They and a handful of other characters are common to most mummer's plays, and to other English ritual dances and songs, as we will soon see. They also represent Pagan themes and teachings.

The Fool begins most mummer's plays by entering the playing area and turning it into sacred space as he sweeps and presumably cleanses the area with his "little broom," a practice not unknown in Pagan circles today. He introduces the other characters one by one and acts as an intermediary between the audience and actors. When St. George, the Hero, dies, the Fool is often blamed, which, as we have seen, takes the death out of the realm of murder and into the realm of the sacred.

In ancient times, the Fool was a mystic, a seer, and people respected his innate understanding of the Otherworld, even as they laughed at his antics. A cloak of almost childlike innocence surrounded and protected the Fool, keeping him outside the laws that governed others. Remember, "God watches over fools" is a very old saying.

The mystical Father Christmas, or Father Yule, is the next to appear. In the world of the mummer's play, he is a proud heir to the ancient powers and authority of the Druid priest. Sometimes Father Yule refers to St. George as his "son," but in a preliterate society, from whence the mummer's play originates, he could also mean "sun." Either word would be appropriate within the context of the play. Not only is the Goddess's son born at Yule, but the sun is "reborn" as the days lengthen.

In some plays, the power and authority of Father Yule is assigned to the character of the King; in others, the King role is combined with that of the Hero, St. George, and is then called King George. In the Sword-Dance Mummer's Play scripted here, the Hero is killed in place of or in honor of someone or something, and it is usually the King.

The first written reference to a man dressed as a horse for seasonal celebratory purposes was at the beginning of the seventh century. St. Augustine of Canterbury had been sent to convert the Anglo-Saxons to Christianity, and a letter from his boss, Pope Gregory the Great, said in part, "If you ever hear of anyone carrying on that most filthy practice of dressing up like a horse or stag, punish him most severely." The totemic Hobby Horse joins the play, an animal that, in Celtic lore, helps the soul journey to the Otherworld after death. But has he come to guide St. George's soul—or our own?

The Hero of the play, St. George, is introduced next. St. George may be the patron saint of England, but according to historical records, he was never an actual person— which may be why the Catholic Church recently demoted him from sainthood. Various ecclesiastical reference books about Catholic saints list different dates for St. George's canonization, dates that span nearly two hundred years. His role here is the Sacrificed Hero or Sacred Substitute who dies and is brought back to life—much like the sun, or the crops. It is also interesting to note that St. George's Day falls on or near the first of May. It appears then that good St. George, patron saint of England, is really an ancient solar deity wearing only the thinnest mask of Christian disguise.

Next to arrive on stage is the Man-Woman, who is St. George's true love. As a man dressed in woman's clothing, this is the most sadly misunderstood figure in the mummer's tradition, even as the character's humorous and bawdy antics make the crowd roar with laughter. The Man-Woman is not, as some modern viewers have suggested, poking fun at homosexuality, transgenderism, or transvestitism by presenting a caricature of a drag queen. The ancient image of man and woman combined into a single being, the hermaphrodite, is one of the oldest symbols of fertility there is.

Moreover, until the late 1980s, the mummer's play was performed exclusively by men, including its female roles (we'll discuss this in more depth later). This has less to do with conscious or unconscious mimicry of the customs of Shakespeare's time and more to do with the traditional attitude, "Well, that's the way it's always been done."

So if St. George is a representation of the Sun God, Blessed Hero and/or the Sacred Sacrifice, then his lover, Bride and Consort is, in fact, the Goddess herself in the character of the Man-Woman. Is it possible that her lewd and comic nature is a result of the deteriorating respect toward feminine divinity over the last thousand years or so?

Slasher. Worm. Pellinore. Thrasher. Beefhump. All names from various times for the Dragon slain by St. George to save his lady-love. Some folklorists have interpreted this story, which is also found outside the mummer's play, as symbolizing the triumph of Christianity (St. George) over Paganism, with the Dragon a symbol of the old Pagan gods—as in fact it is. In ancient Celtic lore, the Dragon, depicted as a horned serpent, symbolized the Crone aspect of the Earth Goddess, and in early versions of the story and the play, St. George subdues the Dragon—or embodies its spirit?—without killing it. So, like the Hobby Horse and the Man-Woman, this is another totemic figure that represents an aspect of the Goddess. Centuries of men playing the Dragon role have made it a he instead of a she, but the meaning is the same.

At the appointed time, the solemn sword dancers, sometimes called the King's or Queen's Men, enter at the Fool's bidding and perform their dance for St. George, ritually killing him at the end. As individuals, they deny any responsibility for his death and blame it on the Fool.

A relatively recent addition to the mummer's tradition and last to enter the playing area is the Doctor, come to "cure" St. George's death. Springing from the same contrary, slapstick tradition as the Renaissance theatrical Fool, the Doctor's efforts are usually ineffectual, and it is old-fashioned magic that eventually restores St. George to life.

The Doctor is the product of a time when country people mistrusted the growing medical profession with its strong Church backing, preferring their familiar herbalists and midwives. Records of various witch-hunts and witch-finders in England show how many innocent "natural healers" were conveniently accused of sorcery and subsequently tortured and killed, thereby reducing the competition. The Doctor character in the mummer's play allowed the country people an outlet in which to strike back at their persecutors in a very small, safe way.

The Mummer's Play: Take a Creative Approach

Mummer's plays are *funny!* Humor is an excellent learning tool, and these plays' original purpose was to convey the seasons' lessons—the cycle of birth, death, and rebirth—to illiterate villagers. Adding topical humor is part of the fun of this living tradition. Feel free to add private jokes and references unique to your group: the performance will be more meaningful, relevant, and funnier for you and your audience. Personalizing the script reflects the spirit of an old and honorable folk custom. Traditionally, most of the lines are rhymed couplets, which are easier to memorize than straight text; this was especially true for a nonliterate society, but it is true for us too.

A few rehearsals are advisable. If possible, gather your cast several weeks early and rehearse four or five times. The goal is twofold: first, to add your own funny references to the script, and second, to give the actors a chance to memorize their lines. (Performing with scripts in hand detracts from the experience for both actors and audience.) On the other hand, don't over-rehearse! Keep it fresh. Another approach is to spring the scripts and costumes on unsuspecting volunteers immediately before the performance, with actors drawing their roles out of a hat. Spontaneity can be magical.

Note for Pagan groups: all participants should ground and center before they begin the play, and personally ground any excess energy afterward.

The Sword-Dance Play

I wrote this play in October 1989, drawing heavily from scripts recorded by folklorists over one hundred years ago, contemporary sources, and my own imagination.

Materials and Preparation: Casting, Costumes, and Props

Costumes may be as simple as a large name card on a necklace cord or as elaborate as you choose. I suggest the more elaborate route, whether your group is fortunate enough to boast a resident seamstress or whether you raid the local thrift shop. It's more fun!

ROBIN JOLLY

The Fool can be played by either a man or a woman. Robin should wear either the classic Renaissance-era jester's tunic or smock with the sunburst "Kermit the Frog" collar and multi-pointed hat, bright clownlike clothes, or tattered raglike clothes—preferably ones that don't match. He or she needs a broom.

FATHER YULE

This role can be played by either a man or a woman. If a woman, emphasize the Crone aspects of the character, both in manner and in dress. My Father Yule wears a large red robe with a white overtunic to symbolize the red sun returning and melting the white snow. I've seen others wear a belted forest-green robe with a hood, which has a nice Victorian look. Avoid Santa Claus costumes. Father Yule carries a tall staff.

HOBBY HORSE

The Hobby Horse can be played by a man, woman, or child. There are two options for costuming. The more primitive and authentic way is to stuff the center of a large sheet or piece of fabric to resemble a horse's head, push an inch-wide dowel into the center of it, and add false eyes, ears, and tail. Then put someone under the sheet, straddling the dowel if it's long enough, or holding it in both hands if it's not. Bear in mind that your actor can't see a blessed thing.

A more complex costume, dating to Renaissance times, is a long full skirt on a frame (a small hula hoop works well), hung from the shoulders with a pair of suspenders. Attach a stuffed horse's head with reins to the skirt, cover the wearer's upper body with a short cape, add a hat, and voila! Horse and rider! (The classic two-person horse known from vaudeville works, too, but remember, your actor still can't see much.)

Although the horse is traditional, your Hobby can be any four-legged animal used to transport humans and/or goods, including camel, unicorn, or donkey. You might find a pre-stuffed head on a stick in the children's toy section of your local farm supply store. Mummers from Missouri might even want to consider a Hobby Mule!

Children love the Hobby Horse. If your group has a young child or two, even if they can't read, you might want to consider casting them as the Hobby Horse. The Horse has only two or three lines to say, and it's a great way to get the kids involved!

Left: An old-fashioned Hobby Horse. He can't see much! Center: A horse-and-rider Hobby.
Right: A classic two-person horse is another option, but again, visibility is limited.

KING WILLIAM

Best played by a man, King William should have a kingly-looking robe, crown, and sword.
I suggest a wooden toy-like sword; it's safer than metal and easy to make. If someone in
your group has small children or works with them, he or she probably has the craft supplies you'll need to make a crown.

ST. GEORGE

This role can be played by either a man or a woman. My St. George wears a navy blue
unbelted tabard with a white quartered circle appliquéd on the front. He too needs a
wooden sword.

GRISELDA THE FAIR

The Man-Woman should be played by a man, preferably one with facial hair, because
(a) it's traditional and (b) it's funny. Be careful who you ask to play this role: a pregnant
partner may result! Griselda will need women's clothes: skirt, blouse, apron, and wig or

hat. Water balloons stuffed into a very large old bra make good breasts, and unlubricated condoms make good water balloons—they're unlikely to break. Lubricated condoms can leave a residue.

PELLINORE THE DRAGON

Pellinore can be played by either a man or a woman. For a costume, repeat the primitive hobby horse idea with a green sheet or piece of fabric. Or make a large green T-shaped tunic for the dragon body. Paint it, if you wish, or glue, staple, or sew pieces of red and/or green fabric onto it for scales. A dragon head can be made of papier-maché, fabric, cardboard, or soft sculpture. Use an old baseball cap as a base to help keep the head in place.

THE KING'S MEN (SWORD DANCERS)

The dancers can be male, female, or a mixed group. They should all dress alike. I suggest blue or black jeans, white shirts, and dark vests for both sexes. They will need their dancing swords. Burnt cork may be used to blacken the faces in traditional disguise: briefly set fire to the cork from your most recent bottle of ritual wine, then rub it on. Burnt cork is easily washed off with soap or facial scrub and warm water, and is far less itchy—and easier to remove—than black make-up or camouflage paint.

DOCTOR STRONG

Doctor Strong can be played by either a man or a woman. The costume includes either a white lab coat over regular clothes, surgical scrubs, or a golfing costume: knickers, sweater vest, ugly tweed golf cap. The Doctor will need a medical bag containing a large nail (for the tooth), pliers, an empty or water-filled liquor bottle, and anything else the imagination wants. Suggestions: pink lawn flamingo, whoopie cushion, dirty magazine, golfing paraphernalia, lacy underwear, bathroom plunger, toy stethoscope or other doctor props, sandwich, bowling pin, kazoo.

Cast of Characters

(in order of appearance)
Robin Jolly
Father Yule
Hobby Horse
King William
St. George
Griselda the Fair
Pellinore the Dragon
The King's Men: six to eight sword dancers. *(If there are six, Dancer 1 takes Dancer 7's lines and Dancer 2 takes Dancer 8's.)*
Doctor Strong

Robin Jolly enters and begins clearing a space with his broom.

Robin Jolly

Room! Make room! Give us room to rhyme!
And we'll show you a play for Winter's time!
Room! Room! Give us more room!

In comes I, little Robin Jolly,
Come with Winter oak and holly.
We are a Winter mummer's band,
Sons of the soil of old England.
Some can't act and some can't sing,
And some will dance a longsword ring.
But we hope your favor we shall win.
Come in, Father Yule! Let us begin!

Father Yule

Ho, ho, ho, ho!
Welcome or welcome not, here I come . . .
Old Father Yule to start the fun.

Yule comes but once a year,
And when it does, it brings good cheer:
Roast beef, plum pudding, strong ale and mince pie,
Now, who likes that any better than I?

Hobby Horse
Me-ee-ee-ee!

King William
In comes I, Lord William the bold.
My sword is steel, my crown is gold.
I am King, and one with the land.
Wisdom and justice are at my command.
Is there any mightier than I?

Hobby Horse
Neigh!

King William
Good Horse.

Robin Jolly
In this room there shall be shown
The fiercest battle ever known.
Here comes St. George, the pure and brave
Who will fight the Dragon to the grave.

St. George
In comes I, St. George, old England's pride.
I am the King's champion, I fight by his side.
Neither gold nor riches do I crave,
But the love of Griselda is all I would have.

St. George bows toward the entrance.

Griselda

In comes I, Griselda the Fair.
Don't you think I'm beyond compare?
I'll try anything once, twice if it's fun,
On matters of love I'm second to none.

St. George

(kneeling)
Madam, I worship the ground you walk on.

King William

Your taste in women is questionable, son.
I've never seen a homelier one.
A bewitching beauty Griselda is not.
The only thing she is, is hot to trot!

Griselda

You should know!

Pellinore the Dragon

In comes I, the Dragon bold,
And Pellinore is my name.
If your blood runs hot, I'll make it cold
A-breathing fire and flame.
I'm looking for my favorite food!

Pellinore stalks the crowd and the actors; all cower in fear, including St. George.

Griselda! You look awfully good!

St. George

Now see here, Dragon, she belongs to me,
A fight to the death I'll have with thee!

Pellinore

Are you serious? A fight to the death?
Save your strength, don't waste your breath!

St. George

To save Griselda, I know I must win,
So I challenge you to battle! Let us begin!

They fight. Pellinore dies gloriously.

Robin Jolly

Well done, St. George! You saved the day!
The Dragon Pellinore is cold as the clay!

Griselda

(kissing St. George)
My hero!

Robin Jolly

Come on, boys, let's remove this beast.
Being dead, he won't mind in the least.

Robin Jolly, Father Yule, and the Hobby Horse drag Pellinore out the door.

King William

Thank you, St. George, for destroying that pest,
When it comes to my champion, I choose only the best.
As you know, I rule this land
By the power of the Lady's hand.
For this great gift she asks a price,
That I give myself in sacrifice.
My death is drawing very near.
The time is now, the place is here.
So I must leave the human race

Unless another will take my place.
So here is the charge I lay upon thee,
Would you die for England, my son, and for me?

St. George

Father, how could you even ask
If I would assume this sacred task?
Of course I'll stand for you at death's door!
What else is a son and champion for?

Father Yule

Here comes a band of the King's Men
From every shire in the land.
These men can dance 'til your head will spin,
And by your leave, they shall walk in.

St. George

St. George must die, and die by swords
That circle round his head.
Dance boys, the sword dance now for me,
For soon I will be dead.

The dancers dance, ending with a lock, which they place around St. George's head. They draw the swords, and he falls.

Dancer 1

What's going on here?

Dancer 2

There's a dead man! Look!

Dancer 3

(pointing at Dancer 4)
Yes, and you killed him!

Dancer 4

I'm sure it's not I who did this bloody act.
It's him that follows me that did it for a fact!

Dancer 5

I'm sure it's not I that did this awful crime.
It's him that came next who drew his sword so fine!

Dancer 6

Don't lay the blame on me, you wicked villains all.
I'm sure my eyes were shut when I saw this man fall!

Dancer 7

How could your eyes be shut when I saw you looking on?
I looked the other way when all our swords were drawn!

Dancer 8

Robin Jolly did this deed and lays it off on me.
Come, rapscallion! Get a sword and I will fight with thee!

Robin Jolly

Peace! If you want to fight, call Mike Tyson.

Father Yule

The death of St. George is very tragic.
He must be resurrected with magic.

Hobby Horse

Neigh!

King William

I agree with the Hobby Horse.
We need a medical doctor, of course.
One who won't charge us too many shillings.

Griselda

And hopefully one who is handsome and willing!

King William

Robin, call me a doctor.

Robin Jolly

All right, you're a doctor.

The King glares, and all characters start searching the audience for a doctor.

King William

Is there no doctor to be found
To cure this deep and deadly wound?

Doctor Strong

Yes, here's a doctor to be found
To cure this deep and deadly wound.
In comes I, old Doctor Strong.
I'm just passing through, I can't stay long.
I'm taking time out from my miraculous deeds.
And I've come to fill your medicinal needs.

King William

Doctor, St. George lies dead.
Killed by a grievous wound to the head.

Griselda

Doctor, you're such a handsome man,
I know you can cure him if anyone can.
You're nicely built, and wealthy, too.
Why, I believe I'm attracted to you!

King William

Tell me, Doctor, what's your fee?

Doctor Strong

Five hundred pounds I ask of thee.

King William

Five hundred pounds!

Doctor Strong

Well, take off five,
If I can't save this man alive.

King William

Tell me, Doctor, what can you cure?

Doctor Strong

All sorts of diseases. Wheezes and sneezes
And anything else my physic pleases.
The itch, the stitch, the palsy, the gout.
Pains within and pains without.
And if a man's got old age in him, I can fetch it out.

Griselda

I'm convinced, you handsome devil.

Father Yule

Wait! How came you to be a doctor?

Doctor Strong

By my travels.
I've traveled to Italy, Sicily, France, and Spain,
Nine times around the world and back again.

I've seen houses topped with pancakes high,
Water so wet they call it dry.
I've done everything that mortals can do.
I'm totally experienced.

Griselda
Me too!

Doctor Strong
Well, enough said.
Let's raise this man from the dead.

Doctor Strong tries to revive St. George with some silly operations—unsuccessfully.

I see the problem! Besides being dead
St. George has a terrible tooth in his head.
This tooth is stuck in there so deep
That it's given him a deathly sleep.
If we all pull together, we might get it free.
Come, everyone! Pull with me!

Griselda grabs the Doctor around the waist and all join in behind her. On the Doctor's signal, they pull, falling backward like dominoes, the Doctor in Griselda's lap, and so on. He shows the tooth triumphantly.

Father Yule
Enough of this! St. George lies dead.
What's needed here is magic instead.

He revives St. George with his staff.

St. George, arise and return to your father!

St. George
Good morning all, my dearest friends.
I'm glad to be awake again!
I was away for a while, now I've returned,
And this is the lesson I have learned:
This holy time of death and rebirth
Brings peace to all of us on Earth.

Father Yule
Now let the music play, and make the sleigh-bells ring!
A sip of wassail punch will make us laugh and sing.
But money in our pockets is a much better thing!
With cheese in our larder and a cellar full of beer,
We thank you and wish you a bright new year!

All collect money from the audience while singing an appropriate wassailing song. See the songs at the end of this section.

Collecting money from the audience is another mummer's play tradition. Mummer's plays were and are considered "bringers of good luck," and contributing to the performance guaranteed the giver some of that luck for the coming year. It is very likely that the cash was and still is spent by the performers at a local pub. Whenever my group performs a mummer's play, we try to give the money to a chosen charity.

—————————————

Just as the longsword dance can be performed without the mummer's play, the mummer's play can be performed without the longsword dance. The focus shifts, though, from the ritual death of the Sacred King to the timeless feud between the Dark Brother and the Light Brother.

The Hero-Combat Play

This story weaves its way through the mythologies of many cultures, and is a symbolic representation of the struggle between life and death, day and night, and Summer and Winter. In the Pagan tradition, the two brothers can be seen as the Oak King and the Holly King, Lugh and Balor, Set and Osiris, and so on. The story even finds its way into English folk song (see "The Two Brothers" in the last section of this book).

For the Hero-Combat Play, St. George sheds his role of sacrificial Sacred King and becomes the Light or Sun God, slain at the waning time of year by the Dark God. Instead of Sword Dancers, St. George has a new adversary. The Turkish Knight was called the Dark Knight in the older mummer's plays; "Turkish" is an unfortunate by-product of the Crusades when the dark enemies (darker-skinned, at least) were the Turks.

This Hero-Combat Play is my own slight adaptation of the Sword-Dance Play, written in June 1992.

Materials and Preparation: Casting, Costumes, and Props

Characters are the same as in the Sword-Dance Play, minus the King's Men and adding a Turkish Knight. The Knight can be played by either a man or a woman, but should be the same gender as the actor who plays St. George, else this deteriorates into a war between the sexes instead of equal but opposing forces. My Turkish Knight wears a belted ankle-length tabard and a Christmas-pageant-type shepherd's headdress. He should also carry a wooden toy-like sword. The rest of the cast is costumed as before.

Cast of Characters

(in order of appearance)
Robin Jolly
Father Yule
Hobby Horse
St. George
Griselda the Fair
Pellinore the Dragon
Turkish Knight
Doctor Strong

Robin Jolly enters and begins clearing a space with his broom.

Robin Jolly

Room! Make room! Give us room to rhyme!
And we'll show you a play for Winter's time!
Room! Room! Give us more room!

In comes I, little Robin Jolly,
Come with Winter oak and holly.
We are a Winter mummer's band,
Sons of the soil of old England.
Some can't act and some can't sing,
But we hope your favor we shall win.
Come in, Father Yule! Let us begin!

Father Yule

Ho, ho, ho, ho!
Welcome or welcome not, here I come . . .
Old Father Yule to start the fun,
Yule comes but once a year,
And when it does it brings good cheer:
Roast beef, plum pudding, strong ale and mince pie,
Now, who likes that any better than I?

Hobby Horse

Me-ee-ee-ee!

Robin Jolly

In this room there shall be shown
The fiercest battle ever known.
Here comes St. George, the pure and brave,
Who will fight the Dragon to the grave.

St. George

In comes I, St. George, old England's pride.
I am the King's champion, I fight by his side.
Neither gold nor riches do I crave,
But the love of Griselda is all I would have.
(bowing toward the entrance)

Griselda

In comes I, Griselda the Fair.
Don't you think I'm beyond compare?
I'll try anything once, twice if it's fun,
On matters of love I'm second to none.

St. George

(kneeling)
Madam, I worship the ground you walk on.

Father Yule

Your taste in women is questionable, son.
I've never seen a homelier one.
A bewitching beauty Griselda is not.
The only thing she is, is hot to trot!

Griselda

You should know!

Father Yule

Come in Pellinore and clear the way!

Pellinore the Dragon

In comes I, the Dragon bold,
And Pellinore is my name.
If your blood runs hot, I'll make it cold

A-breathing fire and flame.
I'm looking for my favorite food!

Pellinore stalks the crowd and the actors; all cower in fear, including St. George.

Griselda! You look awfully good!

St. George

Now see here, Dragon, she belongs to me,
A fight to the death I'll have with thee!

Pellinore

Are you serious? A fight to the death?
Save your strength, don't waste your breath!

St. George:

To save Griselda I know I must win,
So I challenge you to battle! Let us begin!

They fight. Pellinore dies gloriously.

Robin Jolly

Well done, St. George! You saved the day!
The Dragon Pellinore is cold as the clay!

Griselda

(kissing George)
My hero!

Robin Jolly

Come on boys, let's remove this beast.
Being dead, he won't mind in the least.

Robin Jolly, Father Yule, and the Hobby Horse drag Pellinore out the door.

St. George

I fear no Spanish, French, or Turk.

There's no man can do me hurt.

Show me a man that against me dare stand,

And I'll cut him down with my courageous hand!

Turkish Knight

In comes I, the Turkish Knight.

Come from Turkish land to fight.

Far have I come, by land and sea,

There is no man alive who can vanquish me!

St. George

(aside)

In his dreams!

Turkish Knight

Who is this man that dares against me stand?

Who would cut me down with his audacious hand?

A battle! A battle with him, I cry!

To see who in the ground shall lie!

St. George

Thou speakest very brave and bold to such a man as I.

I'll cut thy doublet full of holes and make thy buttons fly!

So stand off, black and Turkish dog! Let nothing more be said,

For if I wield my bloody sword, I'm sure to break your head!

Turkish Knight

I'll hack you and hew you into pieces small as flies!

And send you to the cookshop to make mince pies!

St. George

Here is my sword, now let us battle
And I will make your bones to rattle!

They fight. St. George knocks the Turkish Knight's sword away from him and forces him to his knees.

Turkish Knight

Pardon me! Oh, pardon me I crave,
And I will be thy Turkish slave!

St. George

I will never pardon a Turkish Knight,
So take up thy sword and finish the fight.

They fight some more. St. George falls.

St. George

My blood is spilled by this Turkish Knight.
I die for England, and the Light!

He dies.

Father Yule

Oh, cruel Knight! What hast thou done?
Thou hast killed my only son!

Turkish Knight

But it was he who challenged me!

Father Yule

The death of St. George is very tragic.
He must be resurrected with magic.

Hobby Horse
Neigh!

Turkish Knight
I agree with the Hobby Horse.
We need a medical doctor, of course.
One who won't charge us too many shillings.

Griselda
And hopefully one who is handsome and willing!

Turkish Knight
Robin, call me a doctor.

Robin Jolly
All right, you're a doctor.

The Turkish Knight glares, and all actors start searching the audience for a doctor.

Robin Jolly
Is there no doctor to be found
To cure this deep and deadly wound?

Doctor Strong
Yes, here's a doctor to be found
To cure this deep and deadly wound.
In comes I, old Doctor Strong.
I'm just passing through, I can't stay long.
I'm taking time out from my miraculous deeds.
And I've come to fill your medicinal needs.

Robin Jolly
Doctor, St. George lies dead.
Killed by a grievous wound to the head.

Griselda

Doctor, you're such a handsome man,
I know you can cure him if anyone can.
You're nicely built, and wealthy, too.
Why, I believe I'm attracted to you!

Father Yule

Tell me, Doctor, what's your fee?

Doctor Strong

Five hundred pounds I ask of thee.

Father Yule

Five hundred pounds!

Doctor Strong

Well, take off five
If I can't save this man alive.

Father Yule

Tell me, Doctor, what can you cure?

Doctor Strong

All sorts of diseases. Wheezes and sneezes
And anything else my physic pleases.
The itch, the stitch, the palsy, the gout.
Pains within and pains without.
And if a man's got old age in him, I can fetch it out.

Griselda

I'm convinced, you handsome devil.

Father Yule

Wait! How came you to be a doctor?

Doctor Strong

By my travels.
I've traveled to Italy, Sicily, France, and Spain,
Nine times around the world and back again.
I've seen houses topped with pancakes high,
Water so wet they call it dry.
I've done everything that mortals can do.
I'm totally experienced.

Griselda

Me too!

Doctor Strong

Well, enough said.
Let's raise this man from the dead.

The Doctor tries to revive St. George with some silly operations—unsuccessfully.

I see the problem! Besides being dead
St. George has a terrible tooth in his head.
This tooth is stuck in there so deep
That it's given him a deathly sleep.
If we all pull together we might get it free.
Come, everyone! Pull with me!

Griselda grabs Doctor around the waist and all join in behind her. On Doctor's signal, they pull, falling backwards like dominoes, Doctor in Griselda's lap, and so on.

Father Yule

Enough of this! St. George lies dead.
What's needed here is magic instead.

He revives St. George with his staff.

St. George, arise and return to your father!

St. George

Good morning all, my dearest friends
I'm glad to be awake again!
I was away for a while, now I've returned,
And this is the lesson I have learned:
This holy time of death and rebirth
Brings peace to all of us on Earth.

Father Christmas

Now let the music play, and make the sleigh-bells ring!
A sip of Christmas punch will make us laugh and sing.
But money in our pockets is a much better thing!
With cheese in our larder and a cellar full of beer,
We thank you and wish you a bright new year!

All collect money from the audience while singing an appropriate wassailing song.

Wassail, Wassail (All Over the Town)

The word *wassail* comes from the Anglo-Saxon *wes hal* (pronounced *wass hall)*, meaning "be whole" or "be of good health." To wassail a person was to drink to his or her health and prosperity with more than the usual intent. The wassail bowl was passed around with toasts and song during the Midwinter season's feasting. It was filled with some sort of hot alcoholic drink, such as "lamb's wool," a mixture of hot ale, spices, sugar, and roasted apples to which eggs and thick cream were sometimes added. This bowl was passed among the assembled company; if it was very large, drinking vessels were filled from it. A formal pattern was followed: the master of the house drank first, then the mistress, and so on through the rest of family and guests in order of rank and importance.

Akin to this custom was the carrying of the wassail bowl from house to house. Bands of young people went about after dark, carrying a good-sized bowl decorated with colored ribbons and evergreens. The bowl was usually made of wood, as can be seen in the line from the following song, "Our bowl it is made of the white apple tree."

The wassailers usually sang some version of the wassail song, a cheerful mixture of good wishes and requests for gifts—usually a loaf and cheese, a piece of beef, a drop or two of cider, or everyone's favorite: money.

Early accounts of wassailing indicate that the bowl was full when it was carried around, and those visited were invited to partake. However, in later years, the bowl was taken about empty, and presented at each house for filling with ale, gin, or some other intoxicating liquid. Eventually, even the bowl was forgotten in some areas, and the wassailers went from house to house empty-handed to sing their songs and receive money and other gifts in return. Out of this came the modern-day custom of Christmas caroling.

This version of a wassailing song came from Gloucestershire. It is particularly nice because it has a verse for each aspect of the Triple Goddess familiar to most Pagans: maid (the Maiden), mother (the Mother), and granny (the Crone)! Note: "small" ale had a lower alcohol content—that's why the singers don't want it.

Joyfully

Was - sail,   was - sail   all   o - ver the   town;   Our
bread   it   is   white and   our   ale   it   is   brown,   Our
bowl   it   is   made   of   the   white   ap - ple   tree;   With a
was - sail - ing   bowl   we'll   drink   to   thee.

1. Wassail, wassail, all over the town;
   Our bread it is white, and our ale it is brown,
   Our bowl it is made of the white apple tree;
   With a wassailing bowl we'll drink to thee.

2. Come, butler, come fill us a bowl of the best,
   We'll pray that your soul in heaven may rest;
   But if you do draw us a bowl of the small,
   May the devil take butler, bowl, and all!

3. So here's to the maid in the lily-white smock,
   Who skipped to the door and slipped back the lock
   Who skipped to the door and pulled back the pin,
   For to let these jolly wassailers come in.

4. Come mother, and fill us a bowl of the best;
   We'll drink it down slowly and sing that much less.
   But if you do bring us a bowl of the small,
   We'll wassail the night all here in your hall.

5. And here's to the granny that sits by the fire,
   Come make us some room and we'll sing you an hour.
   We'll sing you an hour, and if you can hear,
   We'll drink to your health, and a happy new year.

Repeat first verse.

The Gower Wassail

This song comes from the Gower Peninsula in Wales. In the words of the final verse, "We know by the moon that we are not too soon, we know by the sky that we are not too high, we know by the stars that we are not too far, and we know by the ground that we are within sound," so the singers know it is the right time for this song.

1. A-wassail, a-wassail, throughout all the town,
   Our cup it is white and our ale it is brown;
   Our wassail is made of the good ale and cake,
   Some nutmeg and ginger, the best we could get.

   Chorus:
       Fol de dol, fol de dol de dol,
       Fol de doldly dol, fol de doldy dee.
       Fol de day-ro, fol de day-dee,
       Sing too-ral-aye-oh.

2. Our wassail is made of the elderberry bough,
   And so, my good neighbor, we'll drink unto thou.
   Beside all on earth we have apples in store;
   Pray let us come in for it's cold by the door.

   Chorus

3. We hope that your apple trees prosper and bear
   So that we may have cider when we come next year.
   And where you've one barrel, we hope you have ten
   So that we may have cider when we come again.

   Chorus

4. There's a master and mistress sitting down by the fire,
   While we poor wassail folk stand here in the mire.
   And you, pretty maid, with your silver-headed pin,
   Pray open the door and let us come in.

   Chorus

5. It's we poor wassail folk, so weary and cold,
   Please drop some small silver into our bowl.
   And if we survive for another New Year,
   Perhaps we may call and see who does live here.

   Chorus

6. We know by the moon that we are not too soon,
   We know by the sky that we are not too high.
   We know by the stars that we are not too far,
   And we know by the ground that we are within sound.

   Chorus

Please to See the King

Hunting the Wren is a ritual that survived well into the nineteenth century in the southwest counties of England, in Wales, and in parts of France. It was still done in Ireland and on the Isle of Man well into the late twentieth century, and may still take place in some remote areas today.

At dawn on the day after Christmas, bands of men and young boys went out into the forest to hunt the Wren. The hunters were armed to the teeth with guns, staves, and hatchets to bring down the tiny, harmless bird. Once captured, the Wren was caged and placed on a large bier decorated with greenery and ribbons, and paraded with much ceremony through the village streets. People gave money, food, or drink to the "Wren Boys" to increase their own good luck in the coming year. At the end of the ceremonies, the bird was set free.

This folk ritual makes absolutely no sense until one realizes that in English folklore, the Wren is a symbol for the King, thus considered sacred, and also considered to be the King of the birds. In older versions of this rite, the Wren was not only hunted, but killed, and his tiny dead body was paraded through the streets on a large, decorated bier. Once again, the Sacred King/Sacrificial Substitute motif appears in the English folk tradition.

The song "Please to See the King" has other versions, sometimes called "The Cutty Wren." It has been recorded by several folk artists.

1. Joy, health, love, and peace be all here in this place.
   By your leave we will sing concerning our King.

2. Our King is well dressed, in silks of the best,
   In ribbons so rare, no king can compare.

3. We have traveled many miles, over hedges and stiles
   In search of our King, unto you we bring.

4. We have powder and shot to conquer the lot.
   We have cannon and ball to conquer them all.

5. Old Christmas is past, Twelfth Night is the last.
   And we bid you adieu, great joy to the new.

Apple Tree Wassail: A Ritual Song and Dance

In this song, instead of wishing good health and fortune to an individual or household, the wassailers encourage the village fruit trees to wake up and grow. This ritual song and dance is best performed near the end of winter in early March, rather than late December, because trees should stay dormant during the worst of the cold season and only be wakened when Spring is near.

Song and Dance Steps

All, with goblet, tankard, cup, or other drinking vessel, take hands in a ring around the apple tree and sing:

Old apple tree, we'll wassail thee, and hoping thou wilt bear;
(Circle to the left 8 steps)

The Lord does know where we shall be to be merry another year.
(Circle to the right 8 steps)

To blow well and to bear well and so merry let us be;
(Into the center 4 steps and back up to place)

Let ev'ry man drink up his cup, here's a health to the old apple tree!
(Into the center 4 steps, salute with drinking vessel, and back up to place)

To blow well and to bear well and so merry let us be;
(Into the center 4 steps and back up to place)

Let every man lift up his cup, here's a health to the old apple tree!
(Into the center 4 steps, salute with drinking vessel and back up to place)

Deck the Hall

Evergreens are still alive even when everything else in nature appears to be withered and dead; thus they have long been regarded as symbols of everlasting life. They were often used in magical rites to ensure the return of vegetation. The three most popular evergreens for these purposes—holly, ivy, and mistletoe—all bear fruit in the winter, and so were regarded as doubly sacred.

Holly and ivy have been linked together for centuries, the holly often being assigned masculine attributes and the ivy feminine ones. Ancient herbalist references speak of them as magically paired. The four cycles of the holly berry (white, green, red, and black) reflect the "four" motif familiar to most Pagans as the four basic elements (air, fire, water, earth), four seasons, four directions, and so on.

Mistletoe is the one holiday evergreen that is almost never allowed inside a church, mainly because it has never managed to lose its Pagan associations. It is the Golden Bough that James George Frazer referred to, not because it is gold-colored (actually, it's a pretty green with white berries) but because the Druids used to harvest it with a golden sickle. The plant was sacred to both the Druids and the Norse people. It was considered a symbol of peace, under which enemies had to cease all warfare, at least for the time being. Also referred to as all-heal, mistletoe is supposed to cure many diseases, promote fertility, avert misfortune, prevent excessive bleeding from a wound, and nullify the effects of poison—which is interesting, considering that the berries are deadly poisonous to humans and animals. It is considered terribly unlucky to cut it at any time but Christmas.

Kissing under the mistletoe is an exclusively English custom and is only found in countries where English settlers carried it. Until well into the 1800s, the English always kissed each other in greeting, even on first meeting. The Kissing Bough, possibly a predecessor to the Yule Tree, is a garland shaped like a wagon wheel suspended from the center of the living room. Decorated with candles, ribbons, red apples, and other ornaments, it was never complete without a sprig of mistletoe hanging in the center. The custom hasn't changed much, for kisses were often exchanged in the shadow of the Kissing Bough.

The custom of bringing an evergreen tree indoors and decorating it developed naturally and gradually from decorating houses and halls with evergreen garlands and wreaths. Trimmed trees were first recorded in Germany in 1605.

In the song "Deck the Hall," the line "See the blazing Yule before us" refers to the burning of a Yule Log. For a very long time, Yule Logs were the most important feature in Midwinter celebrations in Great Britain, France, Germany, Italy, and some East European countries. At dusk the log, usually oak or ash (considered sacred woods even by today's Pagans), was kindled with a fragment of last year's log saved especially for that purpose. It was then allowed to burn continually until the time came to deliberately extinguish it.

The Yule Log was the domestic counterpart of the great communal Midsummer and Midwinter bonfires and festivals. And, like them, it was associated with fertility, continuity of life and protection from evil. The Log also has a more personal significance, in that its flames gave light and warmth to the family dead who, in some areas, were believed to return to their homes at Midwinter, rather than at Samhain.

Time-honored rituals surrounded the bringing home and lighting of the Log. It was generally thought unlucky to buy a Yule Log. If a family had forestland of their own, it came from there. If not, a neighbor's woods usually had the required item. For the Log's homebringing, it was often decorated with evergreens and dragged to the door by a cart-horse or a team of oxen. Those charged with the sacred task sang songs all the way home. Often, corn or flowers were thrown over it and cider, ale, or wine sprinkled on it just before it was lit. As unseasoned green wood, the Yule Log burned long and slow, ideally for the entire Midwinter season, December 21 through January 6.

The Log's ashes and charcoal were used in many places as charms for protecting, healing, or fertility. Sometimes the ashes were scattered over the fields. In Brittany, they were thrown into wells to keep the water pure. Ashes from Yule Logs in Germany freed cattle from vermin and fruit trees from insects. Almost every household with a Yule Log carefully saved an unburnt portion in the home for the double purpose of averting fire and misfortune and ensuring continuity through its use in kindling next year's Log.

Trad. Welsh

Deck the hall with boughs of hol - ly, Fa la la la la   la   la   la   la.

'Tis   the sea - son   to   be jol - ly,   Fa la la la la   la   la   la   la.

Don   we now our   gay   ap - par - el,   Fa la la   la   la la   la   la   la   la.

Troll   the anc - ient yule - tide car - ol,   Fa la la la la   la   la   la   la.

1. Deck the hall with boughs of holly,
   Fa la la la la, la la la la.
   'Tis the season to be jolly,
   Fa la la la la, la la la la.
   Don we now our gay apparel,
   Fa la la la la, la la la la.
   Troll the ancient Yuletide carol,
   Fa la la la la, la la la la.

2. See the blazing Yule before us,
   Fa la la . . .
   Strike the harp and join the chorus,
   Fa la la . . .
   Follow me in merry measure,
   Fa la la . . .
   While I tell of Yuletide treasure,
   Fa la la . . .

3. Fast away the old year passes,
   Fa la la . . .
   Hail the new, ye lads and lasses,
   Fa la la . . .
   Sing we joyous all together,
   Fa la la . . .
   Heedless of the wind and weather,
   Fa la la . . .

SPRING

It is still dark outside when the morris dancers wake on Beltane morning, the first of May. The time has come for the Sacred Marriage, the mystical joining of the Goddess and the God, and the morris dancers know that they must waken the Bride and Groom. The Earth and her children have been waiting for months while the Sun King born at Yule has slowly grown to maturity. Soon it will be time to plant the grain and the other seeds—vegetable, animal, and human—upon which the community depends for survival, and thus will the Marriage be consummated.

Carefully and sleepily the dancers rise and garb themselves in the traditional team outfit or kit—white pants and long-sleeved shirt, brightly colored vest, and a thick sweater to protect against the chill. Grabbing a bag containing the rest of their kit, and perhaps a steaming mug of coffee or tea and a roll, they leave their homes to rendezvous with the rest of the team in the center of town.

Once there, the morris dancers don the rest of their kits. First they tie bell pads to their calves—pieces of leather sporting rows of brass bells and colored ribbons. Next, white elastic armbands adorned with yard-long ribbons are pulled over each bicep, and the dancers try to keep the ribbons from dangling into their half-full coffee mugs. Stuffing two large white cotton handkerchiefs into a belt loop, they listen to the musician tune up in the chilly morning air and jam hats covered with buttons and flowers firmly onto their heads. The Fool arrives in costume, and so do the Man-Woman and the Hobby Horse.

As the sun's edge begins to creep into view, each dancer reaches into the stick bags and pulls out a branch of ash wood about a yard long and two inches thick. They line up in formation and patiently wait for the music to start.

At the first notes of "Drive the Cold Winter Away," they begin to move in centuries-old patterns, pounding their staves on the Earth to wake her. They shake their bell-covered legs and snap their handkerchiefs to scare away the last remnants of winter darkness as they caper high into the air. The double lines come together and clash weapons in the ancient battle of Light and Dark. This time the Light triumphs, for the sun bursts over the horizon in rosy magnificence. The dancers, no longer sleepy, sing out to the world: We did it! The sun has returned! The Earth is awake! I am alive!

That afternoon the maypole with a flower garland crown is raised in the center of town. People young and old, male and female, gather underneath to weave its bright ribbons as they dance in a circle of festive wedding celebration. At the communal feast, all present raise their voice in song to give thanks for the ever-renewing fertility of people, crops, and animals.

Later, in the softness of a May night, in copses and groves on the edge of town, the Sacred Marriage is at last consummated by woman and man, ewe and ram, cow and bull, and Goddess and God . . .

Morris Dancers: Bringers of Good Fortune

Next to maypole dancing, morris is probably the best-known English ritual dance form in Britain and the United States. Pre-Christian in origin, it was very popular during the Elizabethan era and is mentioned in several of Shakespeare's plays. In *Henry the Fifth*, the Dauphin suggests, "And let us do it with no show of fear; no, with no more than if we heard that England were busied with a Whitson morris-dance . . ." (Act 2, Scene 4). In *Henry the Sixth Part II*, York recalls, "I have seen him caper upright like a wild Morisco, shaking the bloody darts as his bells" (Act 3, Scene 1). In *All's Well That Ends Well,* the Clown finds this analogy: "As fit as . . . a morris for Mayday" (Act 2, Scene 2). Shakespeare's favorite comic actor, Will Kemp, was a famous morris dancer of the time, and often performed morris solo dances or jigs on stage at the Globe Theater, although in later years, the term *jig* denoted general between-the-acts entertainment that could include song and ribald poetry—the seventeenth-century equivalent of dirty limericks. Dances similar to the morris in style and content can be found in other countries including Turkey, Hungary, and Spain.

When an entire community's survival depended upon the prosperity of grain crops and animal herds, fertility rituals to promote the growth of those crops and herds, and to increase the number of humans to care for them, were considered a common and necessary part of life. Judging by the time of the year and the trappings (bells, staves, colorful ribbons, white handkerchiefs), morris dancing is a remnant of one such ritual. The white handkerchiefs and clothing symbolize purity. These days most American morris dancers opt for dark knickers. Even if white pants were easy to find in stores, they do show the dirt during an all-day outdoor dance. Shirts, however, are always white and dancers wear either bright vests or crossed fabric baldrics to add even more color to their kit.

Some dances clash staves in battle-like movements that represent the struggle between light and dark or winter and summer. Morris is rarely performed in the autumn or winter months; most traditional teams start their season sometime between Spring Equinox and the end of May, and may dance during the summer, heat and humidity permitting. The staves themselves are naturally quite phallic-looking, which is certainly appropriate for a fertility ritual. Morris bells worn by the dancers jangle to frighten away evil spirits or invoke benevolent ones.

Morris dancers were and are considered bringers of good fortune. Even today it is said that as high as a morris dancer leaps or capers is as high as the crops will grow that year, and modern urban audiences still encourage the dancers with shouts of "Higher! Higher!" As recently as fifty years ago, there were farmers in England who refused to plant any crops until the local morris team had danced around their fields in blessing. When a team chooses a day to "tour," it usually picks three to five places to stop and dance for a half-hour or so. Like their mummer's play brethren, most morris dancers pass the hat at each stop and promise a year of good luck to any who give them money. Again, the cash is usually spent at the nearest alehouse after the day's tour.

In this book's Winter section we met the Fool, the Man-Woman, and the Hobby Horse in their mummer's play roles of innocent instigator/scapegoat, fertility symbol, and conveyor of souls, respectively. Traditionally, any or all of these figures can also be part of a morris team's entourage. Ideally, they are also competent dancers who can replace an injured or exhausted teammate if needed.

If he is the only character present, the Fool entertains the audience. He clowns around with the dancers, pretends to get in their way, and tries to interrupt the flow of dance. If the Man-Woman is also present, she and the Fool act as a couple and are often assigned titles such as Lord and Lady, or King and Queen of May, and are treated with respect and reverence by the dancers. Alone, she flirts outrageously with men in the audience or her teammates. And the Horse character, whether he is a Hobby Dragon, Hobby Unicorn, Hobby Dinosaur, or Hobby Bighorn Sheep, is very popular with small children. Even the shy ones can usually be coaxed to pet his nose for luck or feed him some money.

Women Step Up to the Morris Tradition

One significant and positive change in the morris tradition since the 1980s has been the formation of many women's teams, and mixed teams with both men and women. In the past, morris dancing was an exclusively male privilege both in England and the United States. The same went for mummer's plays, longsword, and the Abbots Bromley Horn Dance. However, maypole dancing and the circular folk or "country" dances have always been a community activity, enjoyed by young and old, male and female together. Surprisingly, these communal country dances are *not* considered ritual dance by modern folk dancers.

There is a logical reason for male-only participation in dances with ritual connotations. Once the people of the British Isles were converted to the idea of Christianity and male priests, they eventually became accustomed to a simple truth: public sacred rites were performed or presided over by men.

Even when the folk traditions explored in this book lost their ritual significance in the eyes of most people, women still did not perform them because, up until the beginning of the eighteenth century, women were prohibited by law to perform in public. They weren't allowed to be bards, actors, or minstrels. Anyone who has seen the 1999 film *Shakespeare in Love* knows the penalties exacted if a woman were to appear upon the stage.

Out in the countryside, however, there were some exceptions. In 1599, Will Kemp took his morris act on the road and decided to dance, not walk, from London to Norwich, a distance of about 107 miles. He kept a diary during his travels, and at one stop related a story about a local female morris dancer who matched him step for step.

But for the most part, male performers dominated the ritual dance and drama tradition until the beginning of the 1900s, when many folklorists and folk collectors, some of them female, created performance groups to demonstrate the newly rediscovered dances and plays. A popular source for willing and able performers was English girls' gym and glee clubs, but they were quickly replaced by young men's groups when the

British educational system decided that many of these dances fulfilled the exercise requirements of private boys' schools.

Things also changed somewhat during both World Wars. The English villages where these traditions flourished often lost their entire adult male population in battle. So the village women morris danced, sword-danced, and staged the traditional mummer's plays to keep the traditions alive—but only until the village boys grew old enough to take their fathers' and uncles' places. The traditions became male-only once again.

Then, in the mid-twentieth century, women began to attend longsword and morris classes at various national dance camps and festivals in England and the United States. If they were truly extraordinary dancers, they were sometimes allowed to teach ritual dance, but there were no women's sword or morris performance teams until the early 1970s, and mixed teams weren't created until even later. In some parts of the United States, women were barred from taking part in all "ritual" classes and performances, including mummer's plays, until the late 1980s. They were, however, permitted to be spectators.

NOTE TO PAGAN GROUPS DOING MORRIS DANCING

I suggest that dancers wear comfortable jeans or sweat pants and sturdy sneakers, and that the more generously endowed females wear a bra! Flowing ritual robes with bell sleeves are neither practical nor appropriate for morris; neither is lots of ritual jewelry. As with longsword dancing, ritual nudity is not a good idea either: sensitive parts (both male and female) can get sore and tired from all the leaping and capering about.

The movements of this dance incorporate the Fivefold Blessing, which sanctifies the five primary parts of the human body used in worship: the *feet* to walk the sacred path of the gods; the *knees* to kneel at the altar of the gods; the *genitals* to create life; the *breasts/chest* to nurture and nourish all life; and the *lips/mouth* to speak the sacred words and pass the religion on to others. These body parts can be blessed by kissing, anointing, or—as in the dance—by simply touching with the hands and handkerchiefs.

Dancers should ground and center before beginning the dance, and then personally ground any excess energy afterward.

Shepherd's Hey Morris Jig: Instructions

In this solo jig with repeated verses and choruses, the bell-wearing dancers step and hop, caper, clap, tap the body, and flip handkerchiefs all in unison, with variations for each chorus. The dancers can sing the instructions aloud as a memory aid, or can enlist non-dancing members of the group to sing the instructions for them. Morris takes a lot of breath!

Materials and Preparations

HANDKERCHIEFS

Each dancer needs two handkerchiefs, traditionally white, one for each hand. They can be made by simply tearing old bedsheets or any fabric into two-foot squares; hemming the edges is optional. The smaller men's handkerchiefs sold in packs at most department stores and discount stores will work, too; so will square scarves or bandanas in any color. When ready to dance, you will tie a corner around the middle finger so that the rest of the material shoots out the back of the hand.

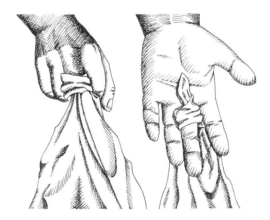

Morris handkerchiefs tied like this are hard to drop.

Left: Anklets can have just a few bells or many of them, as shown here. Right: Bell pads.

ANKLE BELLS OR BELL PADS

Each dancer should also wear bells on both calves. To make a simple bell anklet that can be worn anywhere below the knee, take a nine-inch piece of half-inch-wide elastic, sew the ends together to make a circle, cover it with a sheath of fabric if you wish, and sew four or five bells to the circle. Decorate it with bits of ribbon; a true morris dancer cannot wear too much ribbon! Or you can create the more traditional bell pad. Start with two six-by-nine pieces of leather, one for each leg. Keeping a solid one-inch margin intact at the edges, slit the leather into vertical strips one inch wide. Punch holes in the strips to accommodate the shanks of twenty to twenty-five brass bells. Poke the shanks through the holes and thread them together in the back with string or a shoelace. Decorate the front with bits of ribbon. Attach a three-foot-long strip of carpet binding (or other trim) at the top and bottom for tying it on just below the knee and at mid-calf. Good brass bells are available from the Country Dance and Song Society of America (see appendix A). You can find cheap ones at your local craft store, especially in December.

Preliminaries

- This is a solo dance, but multiple dancers can perform it at the same time.

- If dancers or nondancers are going to sing the accompaniment aloud, divide them into two groups: one to sing the verses (footwork) and one to sing the choruses (hand motions).

- Each dancer ties a handkerchief corner to each hand at the middle finger, letting the bulk of the fabric shoot out at the back of the hand.

The Step

During the verses, dancers move in a small circle, solo, kicking the feet out gently in front of the body, knees relaxed and slightly bent. This is a change-of-weight motion to be executed on the balls of the feet. During the choruses, dancers do hand motions while standing in place, usually gasping for air.

In the sung instructions, "right" and "left" refer to the foot that is on the ground and bearing weight. See Dance Instructions, below, for definitions of action terms.

The Music

This music is in 4/4 time, with a four-bar verse played twice, followed by a four-bar chorus, also played twice. The entire song is played five times through, ending with a final-verse variant. The words are simply dance instructions: "Right, left, right, hop," "clap under, clap behind," and so on, which may be sung aloud.

Morris dancing is traditionally accompanied by a three-hole pipe and tabor, penny-whistle, concertina, fiddle, or button accordion or melodeon (as it's called in England), but any instrument loud enough to be heard over the bells and clapping will do.

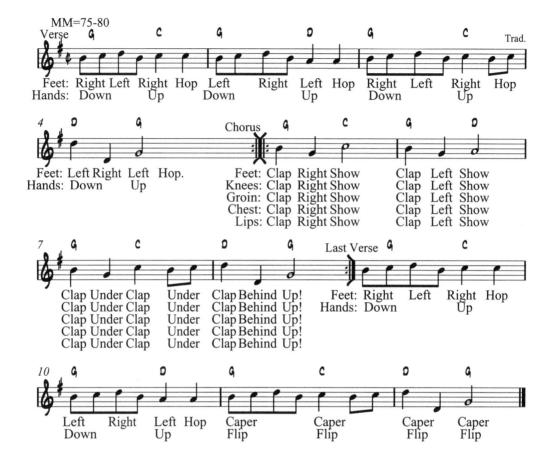

Dance Instructions

Dancers follow the movements shown in the music above, using these actions.

STEPPING ACTIONS

(For the verses, when dancers progress around the performance area)

Hop: Hop slightly off the foot that is bearing your weight, and land on the same foot.

Down: Snap both hands down to your sides.

Up: Snap both hands up over your head.

Caper: Make a lovely high spring from one foot to the other.

Flip: Briskly rotate your handkerchief in a small circle to the side at waist level, something like snapping a towel. Right hand goes clockwise; left hand goes counter-clockwise.

STANDING-IN-PLACE ACTIONS
(For the choruses, when dancers stand in place)

Clap: Clap hands in front of the body one time.

Right: Touch right hand to the body part named in each chorus. Chorus 1: right hand to right foot. Chorus 2: right hand to right knee. Chorus 3: right hand to groin. Chorus 4: right hand to chest. Chorus 5: blow a kiss with the right hand.

Show: Using the hand that just touched a body part, gesture high in the air (pretend you're launching a bird of prey), raising the arm straight up.

Left: Touch left hand to the body part named in each chorus. Chorus 1: left hand to left foot. Chorus 2: left hand to left knee. Chorus 3: left hand to groin. Chorus 4: left hand to chest. Chorus 5: blow a kiss with the left hand.

Under: Clap hands under the knee (lift your foot), right first, then left.

Behind: Clap hands behind the body one time.

LAST VERSE
While the foot and hand motions occur throughout the dance, the caper and flip occur only after chorus 5, to conclude the Shepherd's Hey.

Celebrating Fertility

Equally powerful as an ancient rite but far less complicated than the morris dance is the tradition of maypole dancing. The most common feature of May Day or Beltane celebrations, Pagan and secular, has been and still is "dancing the maypole," which nowadays focuses on the circular weaving of bright ribbons around a wooden pole some ten feet tall.

Because of its shape, the maypole has long been venerated as a symbol of fertility and sexual desire. With its base in or near the earth and its crown pointed up, the maypole can also create a bridge between earth and sky at a time of year when that connection between plowed fields and sun and rain will make the crops grow and prosper. And of course, when the crops grow and prosper, the people and animals dependent on those crops (and each other) also grow and prosper, and the community thrives.

Dancing the maypole is not an exclusively British or British-settled-land custom. In Sweden, the maypole is raised at the Summer Solstice and, like its British cousin, is lavishly decorated with flowers, ribbons, and greenery by the community. The dancing that takes place about its base, sans ribbons, would look familiar to the average English person, although the heart-shaped wreaths that adorn the high crossbar at its top are unique to the Swedish and Swedish-American maypole. Swedish maypoles are also much taller, roughly the height of a telephone pole. The actual raising of the pole is also very much part of the ceremony, and is accomplished by several burly young men aided with guy wires and pulleys.

Maypoles have been decorated with flower garlands and ribbons for many centuries, as period illustrations, woodcuts, and other works of art show us. However, no one actually danced with trailing ribbons in hand until about 150 years ago. It is very likely that the circular folk or "country" dances, which we will look at soon, were originally maypole dances. It is also very likely that budding trees, especially fruit and nut trees, were the original maypoles, minus the artificial decoration. People danced and sang (or chanted, in even earlier times) around such food-bearing trees to bless them or wake them up and exhort them to produce, as in the Apple Tree Wassail noted earlier.

Maypoles also used to be permanent or semi-permanent structures. As recently as the 1970s at Welford-on-Avon and Barwick-in-Elmet, near Leeds, they still were. These permanent poles were most likely located in or near the village or town center, square,

The sixteenth-century enameled glass Betley Window is shown here in a nineteenth-century drawing. Notice the Hobby Horse, the various Fools, and the maypole in the center.

A maypole dance is depicted in this reproduction of an illustration by Joseph Nash (1809–1878). From the Vaughan Williams Memorial Library Collection.

or green. Shortly before May Day they were given a fresh coat of paint and decorated with the traditional crown of flowers and ribbons. They usually lasted anywhere from three to fifteen years before they rotted at the base and had to be replaced.

Most modern maypoles stand eight to twelve feet tall but they used to be much taller, averaging seventy to ninety feet. That height explains why dancing with the maypole ribbons was not part of the original tradition. The ribbons must be twice as long as the pole is high, so that the dancers can (a) get far enough away from the pole to dance without crashing and (b) to weave or otherwise create the ribbon pattern all the way to the base of the pole. So each person around a ninety-foot pole will need 180 feet of ribbon. That's a lot of ribbon! And until about 150 years ago, ribbon was made of silk and was very expensive, something only the nobility could afford in volume. But remember, it was the common folk in the villages who most often danced around the maypole.

Because of its heathenish associations, Oliver Cromwell banned the maypole in England and Wales in 1644, at which time all or most of the permanent poles were pulled down and probably burned. But when Charles II returned and was crowned king in 1653, maypoles triumphantly returned with him. The tallest pole ever recorded stood in London in the Strand on the first May Day of Charles's reign. At 134 feet, it took twelve sailors four hours to erect. Not surprisingly, it stayed there for about fifty years.

The American colonies were also blessed with a maypole in their midst. In 1628, much to the dismay of his Puritan neighbors, Thomas Morton erected a maypole at a place called Merry Mount. Merry Mount was a working plantation in what is now Quincy, Massachusetts, where labor was provided by indentured servants. It was not doing well financially, so the owner, Captain Wollaston, went to Virginia to arrange buyouts of his servants' contracts, taking some servants with him. In his absence, Morton instigated a rebellion among the remaining servants. They removed the man Wollaston had left in charge and agreed to live together as a community, sharing the work and the wealth of the plantation equally amongst themselves and any local natives who cared to join them. And to commemorate the event, they decided to celebrate:

> And upon May Day they brought the Maypole to the place appointed with drums, guns, pistols and other fitting instruments for that purpose; and there erected it with the help of Savages that came thither of purpose to see the manner of our revels. A goodly pine tree of 80 feet long was reared up, with a pair of bucks horns nailed on somewhere near the top of

it: where it stood as a fair sea mark for directions how to find out the way to mine host of Merry Mount.[1]

By all accounts, drinking and dancing about the Merry Mount maypole continued well into the night.

———————————

There are many other May Day traditions in addition to the maypole dance and the May Eve frolic in the woods. May Birching used to be very popular throughout the English countryside. Between sunset on May Eve and dawn, people crept out of their homes and, unseen, attached tree branches or sprigs of plants to their neighbors' doors. This was an effective, albeit cowardly, way to tell your neighbors exactly what you thought of them, as each type of branch or plant had its own symbolic meaning. A sprig of hawthorn tree was always complimentary, and a rowan branch was a sign of deep affection. But a nettle or thistle on the door stated to all, "An unpopular person lives here—and they'd better improve their attitude."

Other plants had symbolic meaning because their names rhymed with particular character traits. A pear branch meant that someone in the house was considered fair of face or fair and honest in character. A person who placed a briar plant on your door considered you to be a liar. Holly was given to persons full of folly but, interestingly, not to jolly people. If a daughter woke to find any sort of nut branch on her door, there would be trouble if her brothers or father discovered who placed it there, because it meant someone thought she was sexually promiscuous—a slut.

Later, May Birching evolved into presenting one's special loved one with a bouquet of flowers first thing May Day morning. Usually the presenter was male and the recipient was female. Most variants of the May Day Carol nicely illustrate this custom. (See the songs at the end of this section.)

Traces of the May Birching and May Bouquet customs apparently came to the United States with early English settlers. These traces survived in America for a very long time, and, in some rural areas, still do. During my elementary school years in Kentucky in the

---

1 From New English Canaan or New Canaan by Thomas Morton. Adapted and spelling modernized by Judy Harrow.

early 1970s, it was customary to weave May baskets out of colored construction paper in art class on May Day. On our way home, my schoolmates and I filled these flimsy, poorly glued baskets with May flowers, primarily dandelions. Often we took them to our mothers, but occasionally we gave them to older women in the neighborhood who had befriended us through the year. The method was amazingly similar to that used by the ancient May Birchers: we hung the basket on the front doorknob, knocked or rang the doorbell, and then ran and hid so that the basket-giver would remain anonymous.

Another traditional activity was gathering May Dew. People, particularly women, went out at dawn on May Day morning to collect dew that had condensed on the grass or shrubs during the night. Common belief held that to wash one's face in this dew significantly enhanced one's beauty. As with so many other folk rituals, this too evolved into another good luck charm. May Dew was also thought to cure many ailments, including tuberculosis, gout, poor eyesight, and spinal weakness. The mother of a delicate child might first collect the dew on a sheet spread on the ground overnight, then rub the dew into the child's groin. This would make the child stronger and hardier. Or something.

Many schools in England have revived some sort of annual May Day celebration, and they often crown a May Queen as part of the festivities. Elected by her classmates, this young girl is either crowned by her predecessor or another "official" individual. In earlier times she was not a girl but a young woman, chosen for her beauty or popularity. A May King was often chosen also, and he presided over the May Day festivities at her side. A Lord and Lady of May were also chosen to serve as attendants. Compare this to the typical prom queen ceremony in American high schools. She, too, is crowned during a Spring celebration, often with attendants. It is possible to speculate that one of our most common high school ceremonies may have its origin in ancient Pagan rites.

It is quite clear, at least, that the choosing and crowning of the May Queen, King, and attendants evolved from the celebration of the Sacred Marriage. This mystical union of the Goddess and the God, from which the fertility of plant, herd, and human springs, is acted out in folk customs throughout history and around the world. In ancient Egypt and Greece, queens were "wedded" to the gods Ammon and Dionysus, respectively. Whether the part of the God was played by a human male or some appropriate substitute object is unknown.

A life-size image of Frey, the Norse God of fertility, once toured the Swedish countryside every year in a much-decorated wagon, accompanied by a young girl who was referred to as his wife. Presumably, she was also his priestess, serving in the temple at Upsala when the tour ended. The people of the villages on their route were generous with offerings of food and drink.

In other places and times, the roles of the Goddess and God were both performed by priestesses and priests. Today, many Pagan groups choose their May Queen and May King by offering small cakes to all who attend their Beltane celebration. Whoever chooses the cakes with special tokens baked inside are the lucky couple. There may be lesser tokens to similarly choose attendants for the royal pair, all of which, as we have seen, is an ancient, time-honored tradition.

Other groups, mine included, offer a series of games designed to test the participants' skill in body (Frisbee toss), mind (Pagan trivia), and spirit (guessing which Tarot card is in the sealed envelope). The highest male and female scorers are crowned the May King and Queen.

NOTE TO PAGAN GROUPS DANCING THE MAYPOLE

For maypole dancing, dressing up in ritual finery and jewelry is appropriate. These dances are usually not terribly aerobic, and they do not involve using heavy or sharp implements, so flowing garments are no problem. However, if the dance is taking place outdoors, the dancers should wear shoes. All participants should ground and center before they begin dancing, and should personally ground any excess energy afterwards.

Maypole Dance: Instructions

In addition to the widely used Weaving figure, this dance includes two less common optional ones, the Barber Pole and the Gypsy Tent/Spider's Web. (Pagans, note that three figures can mean three times the normal amount of energy raised!) If your group is "dance challenged," you might stick to the Weaving figure. This version is based on a routine choreographed in 1986 by my mother, Sylvia Forbes, for the Old Castle Morris and Garland team of Baldwin, Kansas.

Materials and Preparation

CLOTHING

As you may know, "anything goes" is the rule for what people can and will wear—or won't wear—while dancing the maypole! You can't really get too festive when dressing for this activity, but I do recommend shoes, at least! Children might enjoy making masks, wings, or outrageous hats to wear. Pagans, see the "Note to Pagans" on the previous page.

MAYPOLE RIBBONS

Each dancer will need a cloth ribbon twice as long as the maypole is tall: that is, a sixteen-foot ribbon for an eight-foot pole. Consider letting dancers provide their own ribbon: they can choose its color after thinking about what they wish to weave into their lives.

White: Purity, Great Spirit, truth

Brown: Harmony, home, hearth

Red: Strength, sexual forces, courage

Orange: Divination, luck, attraction, friendship

Yellow: Intellect, inspiration, new beginnings

Green: Abundance, fertility, money, wealth

Blue: Emotion, peace, healing

Purple: Spirituality, business affairs

Pink: Self-love, sensitivity

THE MAYPOLE ITSELF

Schools of thought vary on choosing a maypole. Wood is one option, and a natural tree trunk is most traditional of all. If you live in the country, you may know of a sapling grove that needs thinning. (Before you cut it, ask the sapling's permission—and its owner's. Explain your purpose, and be prepared to take no for an answer.) If you are a city dweller, you may have to settle for a trip to the local hardware store to choose your maypole. One option is an eight-foot closet bar: a wooden dowel an inch and a half in diameter.

But some of us object to killing a tree to celebrate nature's fertility and renewal. My maypole is an eight-foot plastic PVC pipe about three inches across, spray-painted brown. Its chemical components do not seem diminish its power. And it has several advantages: its extra thickness helps it fit securely into a Christmas tree stand or a wheel-and-cement stand. Because it's hollow, it also fits over the center pole of a cast-iron outdoor table umbrella holder. Let's look at these options for holding your pole upright.

THE MAYPOLE STAND

If it's not practical to dig a narrow, deep hole in the ground in which to insert your maypole, you will need a maypole stand. **A Yule or Christmas tree stand** makes a pretty good base, and even off-season can be found at flea markets and yard sales, or on eBay. (Replace any missing bolts at a hardware store.) Once the pole is upright and firmly bolted in, fill the bowl part of the stand with rocks or brick chunks to add stability. But stability is relative. Considering the forces of the dance, the pole may tend to tip, and someone may need to hold it. So you might consider a **human maypole base** or at least a human maypole base assistant. (But remember, maypoles are a potent fertility spell. Choose a person who cannot get pregnant, cannot get someone else pregnant, or, best choice, someone who very much wants a child. You have been warned!) Another option is a **metal car wheel** with or without the tire, available at any junkyard. Get a two-foot piece of PVC pipe that fits into the center hole of the wheel, and into which your maypole will fit snugly. Lay the wheel on its side with the pipe sticking out, fill both sides of the wheel to the edge with cement, and let it dry. It's nice to spray-paint this maypole base a dark green or festive color and/or cover it with flowers or budding branches. Another possibility for a hollow maypole, as noted above, is to fit it over the center pole of a **cast-iron outdoor table umbrella holder**—also found at many hardware stores. Although it costs a bit of money, I have found this has the best stability.

ATTACHING THE RIBBONS

But before the maypole is upright in its holder, you must attach the ribbons for dancing. One way is to start with a plain grapevine wreath, available at most craft shops; find one big enough to handle the number of ribbons (dancers) expected. Thread each ribbon between the vines and tie it off securely. Drill two holes all the way through the top of the pole. Tie four pieces of stout cord to the inside of the wreath, then thread

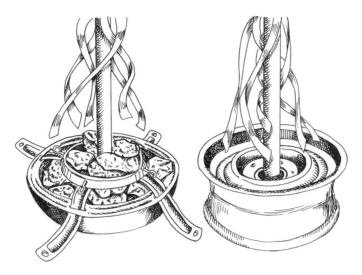

Two Maypole base options: a tree stand and a cement-filled wheel.

them through the holes in the top of the pole and tie them off. If you wish, decorate the wreath with fresh or silk flowers and greenery.

ERECTING THE POLE

When it's time to set the maypole up, I like to ask the men in attendance to do so. It's an appropriate touch, yes?

The Step

An easy walking step is best. Walk, but look like you're dancing! This raises just as much energy as skipping and is easier to maintain for the amount of time it takes to properly dance a maypole—longer than you think.

The Music

Unlike morris or longsword, maypole dancing has no specific traditional music. If the dancers want to make their own music while weaving, choose an appropriate chant or song (see the songs at the end of this section). But be warned: maypole dancers may not have enough breath to dance and sing at the same time! Consider playing recorded music by your favorite Pagan singer or group, or find live musicians or drummers to accompany you. "William and Nancy," a traditional tune in 6/8 time, works very well.

Preliminaries

- Dancers, gather around the maypole in a circle and grab a ribbon, leaving enough slack to dance with but not so much that it drags on the ground. Conversely, do not pull the ribbon so tight that the maypole tips over. Important: Keep holding your ribbon until told to let go!

- Count off aloud by twos clockwise: One, Two, One, Two. Remember your number! Ones, you will pair up with the Two on your right at various times in this dance. Note: An even or odd number of dancers will work fine for this dance—although with an odd number the weave will look a little funky.

Dancing the Maypole: Four Figures, Step by Step

Outlined here are an introductory sequence, the Barber Pole figure (optional), the Gypsy Tent or Spider's Web figure (optional), and the Weaving figure. The "breaks" represent repetitions of the introductory sequence. Less ambitious groups may skip directly from the introductory sequence to the Weaving figure. (Although instructions for all figures are numbered consecutively here, the figures can be done in any sequence.)

INTRODUCTORY SEQUENCE

1. All dancers take hands in a circle (still holding their ribbons) and slip to the left for 15 steps, rest for one beat, then slip to the right for fifteen steps and stop. Drop hands, but not the ribbons.

2. Still facing the maypole, go into the center 4 steps and back out to the circle 4 steps.

3. Each pair (One on the left, Two on the right) turn to each other and bow.

4. Each person turn to the person now behind them and bow.

BARBER POLE FIGURE

5. All dancers face the maypole and go into the center 4 steps. All Twos back out to the circle in 4 steps. All Ones scrunch in close to the maypole, face out, stand still, and pull their ribbon down—firmly, but not too taut.

6. All Twos face left (clockwise) and begin to dance around the maypole in single file. Their ribbons will wind in such a way that the maypole looks like a barber pole.

7. After three or four turns around the pole, all Twos reverse direction and unwind the ribbons. When all Twos are back in place and all ribbons are untangled and even, stop. The Ones now step away from the maypole and return to their original positions.

BREAK

Repeat steps 1 through 4 of the introduction.

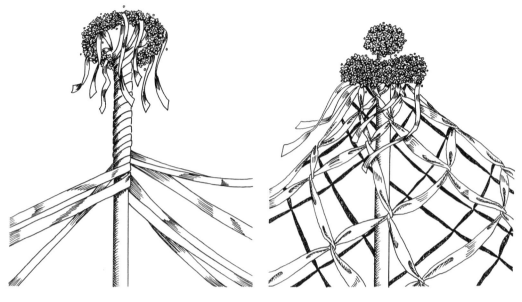

Barber Pole pattern.   *Gypsy Tent/Spider's Web pattern.*

GYPSY TENT/SPIDER'S WEB FIGURE

8. All dancers face the maypole and go into the center 4 steps. All Ones back out to the circle 4 steps. All Twos move about halfway out toward the circle edge and face out, leaving room for your One to dance, fully upright, behind you. All Twos stand still, firmly holding their ribbons slightly over their heads.

9. Each One circles clockwise around their Two, then, moving clockwise around the large circle, continues to the *next* Two and dances clockwise around that person, then to the *next* Two and dances clockwise around that person. Continue for five or six times, then stop and look at your pattern.

10. After five or six more times, all Ones reverse direction and unwind the ribbons. When all Ones are back in place and all ribbons are untangled and even, stop. All Twos now step back out to their original positions.

BREAK

Repeat steps 1 through 4 of the introduction.

WEAVING FIGURE

11. All dancers face the maypole, go into the center 4 steps and back out to the circle 4 steps. Each One and Two pair faces each other around the circle, so that all Ones are now facing clockwise and all Twos are facing counterclockwise.

12. Each One takes one step away from the maypole and each Two takes one step toward it. Important note: do not change directions!

13. Each One raises his or her ribbon. Each Two lowers his or her ribbon. They pass right shoulders with *One's ribbon going over Two's,* then they leave each other behind and continue on to the next person.

14. Each Two raises his or her ribbon. Each One lowers his or her ribbon. They pass left shoulders with *Two's ribbon going over One's,* then they leave each other behind and continue on to the next person.

15. Repeat steps 13 and 14 for a very, *very* long time. Any dancer who runs out of ribbon can tie it off at the bottom of the pole and step out of the circle.

16. Once all remaining dancers' ribbons are interwoven down to the bottom third of the pole, all can stop weaving and tie their ribbons off.

17. All dancers take hands in a circle and slip to the left for 8 steps, then slip to the right for 8 steps and stop.

18. Drop hands, release the energy, ground the leftover energy, and wish your friends a happy Beltane! The dance is ended.

The Wooing Play

All mummer's plays carry the message of death and rebirth, as we saw in the Sword-Dance and the Hero-Combat plays. The Wooing Play is also traditionally performed at Yule but is far more suited to Ostara or Beltane. Its characters try to win the favors of the Maiden Goddess, Fair Elinor, and the Young God, in the character of the Fool, does win her hand at the end. But first the old year's couple, Dame Jane and Old Man, must have their conflict. Thus does the old ever make way for the new. The distinguishing feature here is the Fool's invitation to attend "my wife's wedding." In fact, this traditional speech and the overt wooing, as opposed to the mere flirting we saw with Griselda in the winter scripts, make a Wooing Play what it is.

I wrote this play for my old coven's 1995 Spring Equinox celebration. Based on a traditional script collected in Bassingham, England in 1823, it was likely the first Wooing Play staged anywhere since the 1940s, and the first ever in the United States. The Fool's dialogue with Elinor, and his speech at the end, are verbatim from the 1823 version.

The Wooing Play: Make It Your Own

This play should be bawdy, funny, and filled with double entendres. We must do what we can to encourage the Goddess and her Consort to . . . procreate. Remember, adding topical humor is part of the fun of this living tradition. Feel free to add your own jokes and references, ideally in rhymed couplets, which are easier to memorize than straight text. Rehearse a few times if you can, but keep it fresh. *Note for Pagan groups:* all participants should ground and center before they begin the play, and personally ground any excess energy afterward.

Materials and Preparation: Casting, Costumes, and Props

Again, each character needs a costume and some need props.

TOM TIM TOT

The Fool can be played by either a man or a woman, but for tradition's sake should be the same gender as the person playing Elinor. Tom should wear either the classic jester's tunic or smock and multi-pointed hat, bright clownlike clothes, or tattered raglike clothes—preferably ones that don't match. He or she needs a broom.

FAIR ELINOR

The Man-Woman actor should be of the same gender as the person playing Tom Tim Tot. Elinor needs woman's clothes: skirt, blouse, apron, and hat or blond wig. Remember, water balloons stuffed into a very large bra make excellent fake breasts, and unlubricated condoms make very sturdy water balloons.

FARMER'S SON

The first suitor can be played by either a man or a woman. Old baggy overalls, a plaid shirt, and a baseball cap make an excellent costume.

LAWYER

The second suitor can be played by either a man or a woman. The lawyer should wear an ugly tie, and maybe carry a briefcase.

OLD MAN

The third suitor can be played by either a man or a woman, but should be the same gender as the person playing Dame Jane. In contrast to the Fool's bright clothing, the Old Man should wear dark or patched and worn things. If the actor is not in reality an older man, a fake beard is a must.

DAME JANE

Dame Jane can be played by either a man or a woman, but should ideally be the same gender as the person playing Old Man. Dame Jane wears a dark robe or dress to emphasize her Crone-like aspects, and carries a frying pan and a baby. (The baby can be a doll. At one performance I used an attendee's Labrador retriever puppy. She did a wonderful job.)

DOCTOR GREEN

This role can be played by either a man or a woman, wearing a white lab coat over regular clothes, surgical scrubs, or a golfing costume: knickers, sweater vest, and tweed golf cap. The Doctor carries a medical bag containing pliers (for the tooth) and anything else the imagination wants. Suggestions: financial magazine, stuffed cat (for a "cat scan"), G-string, clown wig, rubber chicken, giant tankard.

Cast of Characters
(in order of appearance)
Tom Tim Tot
Fair Elinor
Farmer's Son
Lawyer
Old Man
Dame Jane
Doctor Green

Tom Tim Tot enters the playing area and begins to sweep it clean with his broom.

Tom Tim Tot
Room! Make room! Give us room to sing!
And we'll show you a play to welcome in the Spring.
Room! Room! Give us more room!

In comes I, Tom Tim Tot
With my great head and little wit.
My head is great, my wit is small.
I will act the Fool's part to please you all.
I have a few jolly boys in my band,
Sons of the soil of old England.
Some can't act and some can't sing,
But our Lady's favor we hope to win.
Come in, Fair Elinor, and let us begin!

Fair Elinor
In comes I, Lady Elinor the Fair.
Don't you think I'm beyond compare?
Some damsels have one suitor, others have two,
But I have three. What's a lady to do?
I wish to marry one and do as I am fit.
So I'll choose the one who best thrills my . . . heart.

Tom Tim Tot
Right.
Come in, lover-boys, and clear the way!

Farmer's Son
In comes I, the Farmer's Son
And heir to all this land.
I hope in a very short time
To win Fair Elinor's hand.

I was brought up at Lindsey Court
All the days of my life.
You are the fairest Lady of all,
I wish you for my wife.

He kneels at Fair Elinor's feet.

With fingers long and rings upon them
Made of the finest gold,
Please, Fair Elinor, marry me.
I would have you to behold.

Fair Elinor
It is my riches you admire,
Not my beauty you desire.
Young sir, be on your way,
I have other suitors to see today.

Farmer's Son exits, broken-hearted.

Lawyer
In comes I, a learned man,
Upon my principle for to stand.
I have come to woo you, Elinor Fair.
To gain your love is all I care.

Fair Elinor

To gain my love, it will not do
To speak too fancy for to woo.
Therefore, out of my sight be gone!
An honest man I'll have—or none.

Lawyer kneels at Fair Elinor's feet.

Lawyer

A man for honesty I am the best!
Lady, please choose me from all the rest.

Fair Elinor

A lawyer I suppose you be—
You plead your cause so eloquently.
But I will tell you before time flies,
I want nothing of a man who speaks only lies.

Lawyer exits weeping, wailing, gnashing his teeth, beating his breast, i.e., not happy.

Tom Tim Tot

Geez, what a sore loser.

Old Man

In comes I, a poor and ancient man,
I do for myself the best I can.
My old grey . . . hairs they hang so low.
I must speak for myself the best I know.
Methinks I see the stars shine bright,
For you, Fair Elinor, are my heart's delight.

Old Man kneels at Fair Elinor's feet.

Dame Jane

Hold it! Hold right there, mister!

Tom Tim Tot

Ohh . . . shit.

Dame Jane

In comes I, old Dame Jane,
A-dabbling down from the meadow.
Come 'round about to show you such sport,
Look behind you, old maids and widows.

Long time have I sought you, Old Man,
But now I have found you.
Come, sirrah, and take your child.

She tries to hand the child to Old Man.

Old Man

Child? Old woman, it is none of mine,
It is not a bit like me.
I am a poor ancient man
Who's just come over the sea.
You never saw me before now, did you?

Dame Jane

I slew ten men with a mace of mustard seed,
And ten thousand men with an old crushed toad.
What do you think of those foul deeds?
If you don't take your child, I will serve you the same.

Old Man

I will be hanged upon our kitchen door
If ever I come near you any more.

Dame Jane

Oh, you will more than hang, Old Man—
I'll answer thee with my frying pan.

Dame Jane whangs Old Man with her frying pan. He falls.

Dame Jane

Five pounds for the Doctor my husband to cure!

Doctor Green

Hey, for five pounds *I'll* be a Doctor!
In comes I, Doctor Green
With cures for ills you've never seen!

Tom Tim Tot

Oh? What can you cure?

Doctor Green

Why, all sorts of diseases
And anything else my physick pleases.
The itch, the stitch, the palsy, the gout.
Aches within and pains without.
You may think I am mistaken,
But I can bring this man to life again.

Tom Tim Tot

Wait! How came you to be a Doctor?

Doctor Green

By my travels.
I've traveled to Italy, Sicily, France, and Spain.
Nine times around the world and back again.
I've seen oceans dry and deserts wet.
(looking at Fair Elinor suggestively)
I'm totally experienced.

Fair Elinor
(*not impressed*)
Yeah, I'll bet.

Doctor Green
Well, enough said.
Let's raise this poor old man from the dead.

Doctor Green tries to revive Old Man with some silly operations—unsuccessfully.

Doctor Green
I see the problem! Besides being dead
This old man has a terrible tooth in his head.
This tooth has been in there so long
That its roots grow all the way down to his . . . waist.
If we all pull together, we might get it free.
Come, everyone! Pull with me!

Elinor grabs the Doctor around the waist and all join in behind her. On the Doctor's signal, they pull, falling backward like dominoes, Doctor in Elinor's lap, and so on.

Tom Tim Tot
Enough of this! This man is not dead but in a trance.
Arise, good sir, and join our dance!

Tom Tim Tot revives Old Man with his broom.

Old Man
Good morning, gentles all, a-sleeping I have been
And such a sleep I've had, the like was never seen.
I saw Dame Jane as a fair young maid
And the sacred grove where we sported and played.
By stars on high and earth so near
I swear this woman is my dearest dear.

They reconcile.

Fair Elinor

Wait a moment—what about me?
I have no suitors when once I had three.
Three have come and three have gone
And left me here lamenting alone.

Tom Tim Tot moves toward Fair Elinor.

Tom Tim Tot

Come write me down the power above
That first created a man to love.
I have a diamond in my eye
Where all my joy and comfort lie.

I'll give you gold, I'll give you pearl
If you can cherish me, my girl.
Rich costly robes shall be yours to wear
If you can cherish me, my dear.

Fair Elinor

It's not your gold shall me attract,
I choose for myself, and that's a fact.
I do not intend at all
To be at any young fool's call.

Tom Tim Tot

I understand, I truly do.
I will put no chains on you.
I'll give you magic, joy, and pride
If you'll be my equal, and my bride.

Fair Elinor

All my sorrow is over and past
My love I have found at last.

This fool who made everything right
Will comfort me both day and night.

They kiss . . . or something.

Tom Tim Tot

I am come to invite you all to my wife's wedding. What you like best you must bring with you, for how should I know what everybody likes? Some like fish and some like flesh, but as for myself I like some good potato gruel, so what you like best you must bring with you.

So let us all to the bridal,
For there will be lilting there.
The Fool's to be married to Fair Elinor
The lass with the golden hair.
And there will be supper and pudding
And bannocks and barley-meal.
And there will be good salt-herring.
We'll relish a keg of fine ale.

All collect money from the audience while singing an appropriate May Day song, such as one from the following pages.

Haymaking Song

In her book *Lost Country Life*, Dorothy Hartley notes that traditionally, "July must see haymaking completed." So it is highly unlikely that the young people in these lyrics are really stepping out to harvest hay "in the pleasant month of May, in the Springtime of the year." That they were slipping out into the fields to celebrate Beltane in a passionate, more *traditional* manner is far more likely, even though one poor fellow appears to be having a rather difficult time of it.

1. 'Twas in the pleasant month of May
   In the springtime of the year.
   And down by yonder meadow
   There runs a river clear.
   See how the little fishes,
   How they do sport and play
   Causing many a lad and many a lass
   To go there a-making hay.

2. Then in comes that scythesman
   That meadow to mow down
   With his old leather-en bottle
   And the ale that runs so brown.
   There's many a stout and a labouring man
   Goes there his skill to try.
   He works, he mows, he sweats, he blows
   And the grass cuts very dry.

3. Then in comes both Tom and Dick
   With their pitchforks and their rakes,
   And likewise black-eyed Susan
   The hay all for to make.
   There's a sweet, sweet, sweet and a jug, jug, jug
   For the harmless birds to sing
   From the morning 'til the evening
   As we were a-haymaking.

4. It was just at one evening
   As the sun was a-going down
   We saw the jolly piper
   Come a-strolling through the town.
   There he pulled out his tapering pipes
   And he made the valleys ring.
   So we all put down our rakes and forks
   And we left off haymaking.

5. We call-ed for a dance
   And we trip-ped it along.
   We danced all round the haycocks
   'Til the rising of the sun.
   When the sun did shine such a glorious light
   How the harmless birds did sing.
   Each lad he took his lass in hand
   And went back to his haymaking.

Padstow May Song

When seen in a mummer's play or as a morris dance onlooker, the Hobby Horse plays a small and silent or near-silent role. But when he appears in the streets of Padstow, Cornwall, on May Eve and May Morning, the "Old Oss" is the star of the show, the one people have gathered together for centuries to see. He is a frightening creature, constructed of a heavy hoop about six feet across, covered with a black canvas skirt. Unlike the horse-and-rider Hobby, whose skirted hoop hangs at waist level, the man inside the Old Oss wears his hoop at shoulder level and a hooded mask of black, white, and red covers his face. A black wooden Hobby Horse head with snapping jaws is attached to the front of the hoop, and a false tail hangs at the back.

At midnight on May Eve, the Old Oss emerges from his winter home behind the Golden Lion Inn and, accompanied by the "Ossy Choir," makes his rounds through the village of Padstow. The revelers stop at various houses and sing the Night Song (verses six through thirteen below, beginning with "Rise up . . ."). Inserting names of specific people in your group or community would be very appropriate here.

Early the next morning, the townspeople cry out "Oss, Oss, Wee [our] Oss!" as the Old Oss again appears in the streets of Padstow for the annual processional through town. He is preceded by the Teaser, dressed as either a sailor or a Fool, who carries a very phallic-looking club. The townspeople sing the May Day Song (verses one through five below) as the Old Oss and the Teaser dance in the streets. Occasionally the Old Oss will chase and catch a young unmarried girl under his skirt, ensuring that she will be married by year's end, according to tradition. Long ago, the Oss's skirt was covered with tar and he carried a bag of soot for marking the girl as a sign of the good luck or fertility to come, but this has not been done since about 1930.

When the townsfolk sing the Dirge, the Oss sinks to the ground and dies a magical death. At the end of the Dirge, the Teaser swats the Oss with his phallic club, the Oss leaps up into the air with renewed vigor, and the procession and singing continues.

The reference to St. George in the Dirge implies that the Padstow rite has a strong connection with our now-familiar Solar Deity, whose Saint's Day is on or about May 1. "He's out in his long boat all on the salt seas, O" may very likely refer to a funeral ship, and so refer to the death and rebirth of St. George and/or the Old Oss. In England in the distant past, it was often the custom to place an important dead body in a ship with all his or her worldly goods, up to and occasionally including livestock, human servants, and spouse, and put it to sea or bury it in the ground. Sometimes the seafaring ship was set ablaze before it left.

The reference to Aunt Ursula Birdhood in the Dirge probably alludes to the Saxon Bear-Goddess Ursel. Ursa Major, the Big Dipper constellation, is often called the Great Bear. Ursel is another deity, this time a Moon Goddess, who was canonized and made Saint Ursula by early Christians.

1. Unite and unite and let us all unite
   For summer is a-comin' today.
   And whither we are going, we all will unite
   In the merry Morning of May.

2. The young men of Padstow, they might if they would
   For summer . . .
   They might have built a ship and gilded it with gold
   In the merry . . .

3. The young maids of Padstow they might if they would
   They might have made a garland of the white rose and the red.

4. Where are the young men that now here would dance?
   Some they are in England and some they are in France.

5. Where are the young maids that now here would sing?
   They are in the meadow a-flower gathering.

   Dirge:
   O, where is St. George? O where is he now?
   He's out in his long boat all on the salt seas, O.
   Up flies the kite. Down falls the lark, O.
   Aunt Ursula Birdhood, she had an old yowe,[2]
   And she died in her own park, O.

6. Rise up, Mr. _____, and joy you betide.
   And bright is your bride that lies by your side.

7. Rise up, Mrs. _____, and gold be your ring,
   And give us some ale, the merrier we shall sing.

8. Rise up, Mr. _____, and reach me your hand,
   And you shall have a lively lass with a thousand pounds in hand.

---

2 yowe: ewe.

9. Rise up, Miss _____, all out of your bed,
   You chamber shall be strewed with the white rose and the red.

10. Rise up, Mr. _____, I know you well and fine.
    You have a shilling in your purse and I wish it was in mine.

11. Rise up, Miss _____, all in your gown of green,
    You are as fine a lady as waits upon the Queen.

12. Rise up, Miss _____, and strew all your flowers.
    It is but a while ago since we have strew-ed ours.

13. Rise up, Mr. _____, with your sword by your side.
    Your steed is in the stable awaiting for to ride.

14. Now we fare you well and we bid you all good cheer.
    We'll call no more unto your house before another year.

Hal An Tow

Furry Day at Helston in Cornwall is probably the oldest example of a communal spring rite still performed in England. The festival takes place on or about May 8, and the local people claim that it has been an annual event for centuries.

The townsfolk spend many weeks painting, whitewashing, and generally cleaning up the town to prepare for the big day. On Furry Day itself, houses and public buildings are decorated with budding branches, flowers, and evergreens.

The day's festivities begin with the Early Morning Dance, which is primarily for the young people of Helston. They process through the town, the girls dressed in white with garlands in their hair and the boys dressed as St. George, Robin Hood, Friar Tuck, or Little John. At certain fixed points, they stop to sing the ancient song "Hal An Tow." The dancing and festivities then continue all day and late into the night.

The most remarkable thing about Helston Furry Day is how little it has altered with time. It remains a communal festival in the truest sense; everyone from the mayor down to the youngest school child takes part. The festival's ancient origins show clearly in the spring cleaning and decorating activities, in the words of the traditional song, and in the never-omitted luck-bringing visits to friends and neighbors.

Many folklorists have argued over the meaning of the words *hal an tow.* One theory holds that it is a Cornish adaptation of "heave on the rope" in the Dutch language. In 1660 it was reported that men setting up a maypole in Newlyn were singing "Haile and Taw and Jolly Rumbelow." *Hal an ta* means "hoist the roof" in old Cornish. One may very well have to heave on the rope and hoist the roof to set up a seventy-foot maypole! Or, since this song accompanies a procession of dancers, *hal an tow* could also refer to a heel-and-toe step in the dance.

The words of the first verse tell us, "Take no scorn to wear the horn. It was the crest when you were born. . . ." Positions on traditional dance teams were handed down from father to son or uncle to nephew: this was true for morris, longsword, and the Abbots Bromley Horn Dance. And it is rumored that in the old traditional covens, the positions of High Priest and Priestess were also handed down along family lines. In many Pagan groups, the High Priest wears a crown of antlers for special occasions.

Rollicking

Take no scorn to wear the horn, It was the crest when you were born. Your

fath - er's fath - er wore it, And your fath - er wore it too.

Hal - an - tow. Jol - ly rum - ble O. We were up

long be-fore the day O, To wel-come in the sum - mer, To wel-come in the

May O, For sum-mer is a com-in' in and win-ter's gone a - way O.

1. Take no scorn to wear the horn.
   It was the crest when you were born.
   Your father's father wore it,
   And your father wore it too.

   Chorus:
   Hal-an-tow, jolly rumble, O.
   We were up long before the day, O,
   To welcome in the summer,

To welcome in the May, O.
For summer is a-comin' in
And winter's gone away, O.

2. Robin Hood and Little John,
   They've both gone to the fair, O.
   And we will to the merry green wood
   To hunt the buck and hare, O.

   Chorus

3. What happened to the Spaniards
   That made so great a boast, O?
   They shall eat the feathered goose
   And we shall eat the roast, O.

   Chorus

4. God bless Aunt Mary Moses
   In all her power and might, O.
   And send us peace to England,
   Send peace both day and night, O.

   Chorus

May Day Carol

Across America, a few high schools and junior high schools are fortunate enough to have an English, Danish, and/or American folk dance team. Every spring these teams come together in my hometown of Berea, Kentucky, for several days of workshops, classes, and dance parties, ending with a public performance on Saturday night.

The dancers—hundreds of them—process into the hall in a long line of couples, each couple holding hands, and each free hand holding a small sprig of newly blossomed forsythia bush or redbud tree. They hold these small emblems of spring high above their heads as the line becomes a spiral and they pause in their processional to turn, skip, and dance under arches made by the neighboring couples. When all have entered, the dance music stops, and everyone on the floor turns out toward the audience to sing the "May Day Carol." The dancers then give their flowering twigs to audience members, and the performance continues.

This song may have its origins in the May Birching tradition, but its message is more personal and deliberate. It is easy to visualize standing on a doorstep or front porch on Beltane morning singing this song for a special beloved, presenting a small bouquet of flowers, too.

Most songs named "May Day Carol" have identical or similar lyrics to the version shown here. Since the lyrics specify no particular Lord or God, I feel it is acceptable for the Pagan repertoire. The singer can be invoking the Lord of the Forest or the God of Growing Things, keeping the traditional words intact, or the words Lady and Gods can be substituted instead.

1. I've been a-wand'ring all the night,
   And the best part of the day.
   Now I'm returning home again.
   I bring you a branch of May.

2. A branch of May, my love, I say
   As at your door I stand.
   It's nothing but a sprout, but it's well budded out
   By the work of the Lord's own hand.

3. In my pocket I've got a purse
   Tied up with a silver string.
   All that I do need is a bit of silver
   To line it well within.

4. My song is done and I must be gone.
   I can no longer stay.
   God bless you all both great and small
   And send you a joyful May.

Come Lasses and Lads

Here is a delightful description of some young couples as they dance around the village maypole and celebrate the return of spring. If you grew up watching Warner Brothers cartoons, as I did, you'll remember the song from the episode with Daffy Duck as Robin Hood, complete with lute, and Porky Pig as Friar Tuck.

1. Come lasses and lads, take leave of your dads,
   And away to the maypole hie.
   For ev'ry fair has a sweetheart there
   And a fiddler standing by.
   Then Willie will dance with Jane,

And Johnny has got his Joan.
And ev'ry maid shall trip it, trip it, trip it up and down,
And ev'ry maid shall trip it, trip it, trip it up and down.

2. "Let's start," says Dick. "Aye, aye," says Nick,
"And I prithee, fiddler, play."
"Agreed," says Hugh, and so says Sue,
"For this is a holiday."
Then every lad did doff
His hat unto his lass,
Then ev'ry maid did curtsey, curtsey, curtsey on the grass,
Then ev'ry maid did curtsey, curtsey, curtsey on the grass.

3. "Begin," says Matt. "Aye, aye," says Nat,
"We'll lead up 'Packington's Pound.'"
"No, no," says Nolly, and so says Dolly,
"We'll first have 'Sellenger's Round.'"
Then every man began
To foot it round about.
And ev'ry maid did step it, step it, step it in and out,
And ev'ry maid did step it, step it, step it in and out.

4. "You're out!" says Dick. "Not I," says Nick,
"'Twas the fiddler played it wrong."
"'Tis true," says Hugh, and so says Sue,
And so says everyone.
The fiddler then began
To play the tune again.
And ev'ry maid did jig it, jig it, jig it to the men,
And ev'ry maid did jig it, jig it, jig it to the men.

5. "Let's kiss," says Jan. "Aye, aye," says Nan,
And so says every she.
"How many?" says Nat. "Why, three!" says Matt,
"For that is a maiden's fee."

The men instead of three
Did give them half a score.
And the maids in kindness, kindness, kindness give 'em as many more,
And the maids in kindness, kindness, kindness give 'em as many more.

6. Well there they did stay for the whole of the day,
   And they tired the fiddler quite,
   With dancing and play without any pay
   From morning until night.
   They told the fiddler then
   They'd pay him for his play.
   And each a tuppence, tuppence, tuppence give him and went away,
   And each a tuppence, tuppence, tuppence give him and went away.

7. "Goodnight!" says Harry. "Goodnight!" says Mary.
   "Goodnight!" says Dolly to John.
   "Goodnight!" says Sue to her sweetheart Hugh.
   "Goodnight!" says everyone.
   Some walked and some did run,
   Some loitered on the way.
   And they bound themselves with kisses twelve to meet next holiday,
   And they bound themselves with kisses twelve to meet next holiday.

Nuts in May

This traditional singing game from Kent is an excellent activity for children at a Beltane picnic or feast. Adults may enjoy it too! The game depicts marriage by contract, and most likely comes from a time when communities made agreements about who would go as a bride from one to the other. In this game, traditionally a girl is chosen to be "nuts in May" and a boy is chosen to "fetch her away." But the distinction isn't necessary, and children will probably have more fun if they can fetch whomever they want. Make sure all children playing are chosen at least once.

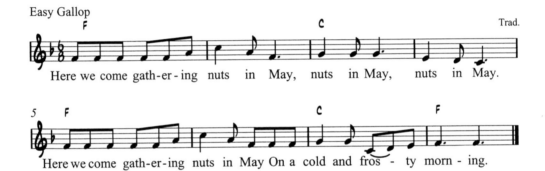

1. Here we come gathering nuts in May,
    Nuts in May, nuts in May.
    Here we come gathering nuts in May
    On a cold and frosty morning.

2. Who will you have for nuts in May? . . .

3. We'll have *[child's name]* for nuts in May . . .

4. Who will you have to fetch her away? . . . (or "fetch him away")

5. We'll have *[child's name]* to fetch her away . . . (or "fetch him away")

Nuts in May: Singing and Dancing Instructions

Children form two lines facing each other (Line A and Line B) with about six feet of dancing space in between.

Verse 1: Both lines skip forward toward each other as they sing the first line, then back to place as they sing the second, forward for the third, and back for the fourth.

Verse 2: Line A advances, asking "Who will you have for nuts in May?" then goes back to place, as above. Repeat.

Verse 3: Line B chooses a child from Line A and advances, singing "We'll have *[name]* for nuts in May," then goes back to place. Repeat.

Verse 4: Line B advances again, asking "Who will you have to fetch her/him away?" then goes back to place. Repeat.

Verse 5: Line B chooses a child from Line A and advances, singing "We'll have *[name]* to fetch her/him away," then goes back to place. Repeat.

The singing pauses. The two chosen children face each other, toeing a mark or line on the ground. They clasp hands, arm-wrestling style, and each tries to pull the other off balance to step over the mark. Whoever is pulled over loses. The loser and the victor both go to the victor's side, and the game continues until one side has all the players.

Alternate the questioning and the choosing each time the sequence is repeated. That is, the next time, on verse 2 Line B advances and asks the question; on verse 3 Line A chooses a child from Line B, and so on.

SUMMER

The longest day's shadows stretch their fingers across the meadow as people gather to light the Midsummer bonfire. It is a festive time, sometimes the only chance for neighbors and friends who are busy from dawn to dusk with crops and livestock to gossip, play, and relax. Everyone has brought food aplenty, a harbinger of the coming harvest, and a stick of wood or twist of straw to add to the growing pile.

At sundown the bonfire is lit. All present, young and old, male and female, join hands and dance in a circle around it. Into the center they skip, faces aglow in the ruddy light. The men join hands and step in one direction while the women step the other. Partners bow, then one circles about the other in the oldest dance of courtship. The musicians stand to one side—a fiddle, a pipe, perhaps some drums. Young people leap over the bonfire's wild flames, hoping to increase their luck in the coming year. Loving couples do the same, their hands linked tightly. Later, when the flames are a sea of low embers, the older couples skip safely over it. When the dance ends, the feast begins. Meat, fruits and fresh vegetables, cider and ale: all is in plenty.

Afterward, the revelers are more mellow, and some of their own step forward in homemade costumes and blackened faces to reenact a story of the Lord of Summer, Jack-of-the-Green in his Robin Hood persona. In the warm light of the crackling flames, children boo loudly when the Sheriff of Nottingham plots his evil doings, and when the play is ended, everyone willingly offers a coin to the merry band.

The mighty bonfire is a sleeping lion of embers when the celebration ends. Slumbering infants are quietly lifted, empty baskets are collected, and one young woman lifts her voice in song to help guide the weary travelers to their beds.

Is this a Midsummer celebration from hundreds of years ago, or a scene enacted at modern Pagan festivals across America every June and July?

Or, again, could it possibly be both?

Country Dancing: All Gather

England's time-honored social dances, or country dances, are the only ritual dance activity traditionally shared by men, women, and children alike. They are the ancestors of American square dancing, the Virginia Reel, and that unique dance-child born of New England, contra dancing. As a form of sacred dance, these are among the easiest. They are not nearly as physically taxing as morris, nor as complicated and entangling as longsword. Like all other English ritual dances, they are structured much like folk songs with a figure (or verse), then a chorus, then another figure, then the same chorus.

Many of England's country dance songs were first printed between 1652 and 1728 by the London publisher John Playford and his descendants. But they had been practically forgotten by the time they were rediscovered by folklorists in the early 1900s.

One of the most common formations for these dances is the circle. A maypole most likely occupied the center of these circle dances for centuries, but it is easy to visualize that place of honor held by an altar, a newly married couple, a bonfire, or a visiting dignitary, depending on the occasion. According to Cecil Sharp, one of the early folklorists responsible for the survival of the country and other ritual dances:

> Although it has for many generations been danced purely as a means of social and artistic recreation, it had its origin in the processional and ring dances which at one time formed part of the May Day ritual . . . It was, and so far as it is practiced it still is, the ordinary, everyday dance of the country-folk, performed not merely on festal days, but whenever opportunity offered and the spirit of merrymaking was abroad.[1]

Therefore, the country dance is not nearly as seasonally bound as its longsword and morris brethren, and is an appropriate part of any seasonal celebration. One modern example: in my home town of Berea, Kentucky, a folk dance and music workshop week has been held between Christmas and New Year's Day every year since 1938. At midnight on New Year's Eve, after an evening of entertainment that includes dance, song,

---

1 This passage appears in Cecil Sharp's *Country Dance Book Volume 1,* which was published in 1909.

and a mummer's play, all the participants gather on the largest floor, with the musicians in the center, and dance in the New Year. The country dance chosen for this auspicious moment is "Sellenger's Round," also known as "The Beginning of the World."

NOTE TO PAGAN GROUPS DOING COUNTRY DANCING

Here are two more dances with leeway for dress, the more colorful the better. Wear flowing robes or Renaissance costume or go skyclad (but wear shoes if dancing outdoors!). As always, ground and center first, and ground any excess energy afterward.

Sellenger's Round

Also called "The Beginning of the World," this merry dance can be done by as few as six people or as many as six hundred. It is danced in pairs, traditionally referred to as couples, standing side by side in a large circle, facing in. These pairs can comprise a man and a woman, or two people from the same gender; it truly does not matter.

The Step

Aside from some specific quick footwork, the step should be a graceful, easy walking step with most of the weight on the balls of the feet.

Music

In 6/8 time, this traditional tune has five eight-bar verses, each followed by an eight-bar chorus. Typical instruments might include some mix of fiddle, piano, recorder, whistle, accordion, and concertina. The dance figures are shown here beat by beat.

MM=96-100 — Trad.

1. Hands, slip to the left for eight steps and stop.
2. Hands, to the center four steps and back.
3. Side with your partner over and back.
4. Arm right your partner all the way around.
5. Hands slip to the left for eight steps and stop.

1. Hands slip to the right for eight steps and stop.
2. Hands, to the center four steps and back.
3. Side with your partner over and back.
4. Arm left your partner all the way around.
5. Hands, slip to the right for eight steps and stop.

Chorus: (1-5) Set into the center, four steps, back to place.

Set to your partner right and left, turn single.

Dance Instructions

After practicing the figures outlined below, follow them as shown in the music.

Hands: Join hands at about waist level with the dancers on both sides of you.

Slip: Take 8 slipping steps sideways to the right or left, as noted.

Set or Setting: In this 4-beat hesitation-like move, you step and quickly shift your weight from foot to foot, either right-left-right or left-right-left, moving your body *slightly* from side to side. You can do this in place or while moving.

Turn single: In 4 beats, turn yourself around in 4 small steps, following your right shoulder around. You can do this in place or while moving.

Siding: Face your partner, take left hands and pull past each other, then let go and turn around: you have traded places in 4 beats. Then take right hands and trade back. Now do it without hands: the no-hands version is called siding.

Arming: Facing your partner, link right elbows, circle each other in 8 beats and return to place. This is "arm right." Link left elbows for "arm left."

Gathering Peascods

Like Sellenger's, this is a group dance "for as many as will," with couples forming a large circle facing in. Irrespective of actual gender, the person on the *left* side of each pair is referred to here as the man; the person on the *right* as the woman.

The Step

Again, like Sellenger's, the step is a graceful, easy walking step with most of the weight on the balls of the feet.

Music

This tune is in 4/4 time, with four 8-bar verses followed by a 16-bar chorus. As in "Sellenger's Round," typical instruments include fiddle, piano, recorder, whistle, accordion, and concertina.

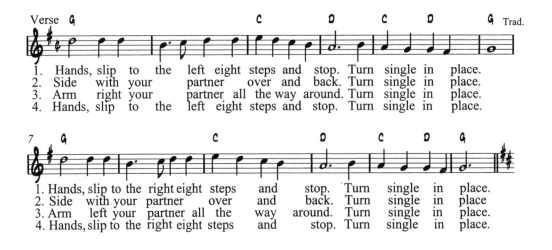

Verse
1. Hands, slip to the left eight steps and stop. Turn single in place.
2. Side with your partner over and back. Turn single in place.
3. Arm right your partner all the way around. Turn single in place.
4. Hands, slip to the left eight steps and stop. Turn single in place.

1. Hands, slip to the right eight steps and stop. Turn single in place.
2. Side with your partner over and back. Turn single in place
3. Arm left your partner all the way around. Turn single in place.
4. Hands, slip to the right eight steps and stop. Turn single in place.

13 Chorus

1.Men: hands & slip around inside   the circle as far as you can, &   back   up to
2.Women: hands & slip around inside   the circle as   far as you can, &   back   up to
3.Men: hands & slip around inside   the circle as   far as you can, &   back   up to
4.Women: hands & slip around inside   the circle as   far as you can, & back   up to

20

place. Women: hands & slip around   inside the circle as far as you can, & back   up to
place. Men: hands & slip around   inside the circle as far as you can, & back   up to
place. Women: hands & slip around   inside the circle as far as you can, & back   up to
place. Men: hands & slip around   inside the circle as far as you can, & back   up to

26

place.   And men   to the center & clap. And women to the center and clap. And
place.   And women to the center & clap. And men   to the center and clap. And
place.   And men   to the center & clap. And women to the center and clap. And
place.   And women to the center & clap. And men   to the center and clap. And

men   to the center & clap,   turn   single   back   to place.   Women
women to the center & clap,   turn   single   back   to place.   Men
men   to the center & clap,   turn   single   back   to place.   Women
women to the center & clap,   turn   single   back   to place.   Men

5

to   the   center   &   clap,   men   to   the   center   and   clap,
to   the   center   &   clap,   women to   the   center   and   clap,
to   the   center   &   clap,   men   to   the   center   and   clap,
to   the   center   &   clap,   women to   the   center   and   clap,

9

women to   the   center &   clap.   Turn   single   back to   place.
men   to   the   center &   clap.   Turn   single   back to   place.
women to   the   center &   clap.   Turn   single   back to   place.
men   to   the   center &   clap.   Turn   single   back to   place.

Instructions

As in the previous dance, follow the instructions shown in the music above after practicing the figures described here. (Other than "To the center and clap," all these moves are also used in Sellenger's Round. Note the details under "Slip" for this dance.)

To the center and clap: Take 4 steps into the center of the circle, clap your hands once and back up 4 steps as the other "gender" takes 4 steps into the center of the circle to clap once.

Hands: Join hands at about waist level with the dancers on both sides of you.

Slip: Take 7 slipping steps sideways to the right or left, as noted. Note: During the choruses, women join hands and slip around an inner circle in one direction, the men also do so. If the circle is larger than five couples, *do not* try to slip all the way around this inner circle. You won't make it. Simply fall back into the circle and pray your partner ends up beside you—and on the correct side.

Set or Setting: In this 4-beat hesitation-like move, you step and quickly shift your weight from foot to foot, either right-left-right or left-right-left, moving your body *slightly* from side to side. You can do this in place or while moving.

Siding: Facing your partner, take left hands and pull past each other, then let go and turn around: you have traded places in 4 beats. Then take right hands and trade back. Now do it without hands: the no-hands version is called siding.

Arming: Facing your partner, link right elbows, then circle each other for 8 beats and return to place. This is "arm right." Link left elbows and do the same for "arm left."

Robin Hood: Outlaw, Folk Hero, Green Man

Although many references to Robin Hood Plays can be found across England in old town records, diaries, and depictions of May Day celebrations, only tiny fragments of the texts of these plays have survived to modern times. The fragments that do exist often echo, or even repeat verbatim, various ballads about Robin Hood, Little John, and the rest of the Merry Men, ballads of which there are legion. The Robin Hood Play tradition appears to have died out about four hundred years ago.

But who was Robin Hood, really?

As with his soul-brother, St. George, it is unlikely that a single, historical person named Robin Hood ever actually existed. Many writers assume that he and his fellow Merry Men are characters that blend the remains of ancient Pagan beliefs with the later exploits of very real outlaws, none of whom were actually named Robin Hood.

It has been suggested that Robin Hood, or "Robin with a Hood," was a title given to Pagan priests, possibly those who worshiped a particular aspect of the Horned God called Robin Goodfellow—a name later associated with the Devil by the Inquisitors. Robin, as the Horned God, ruled over the forests, and thereby over the people and animals who lived within them and survived on the forest's bounty.

Later, real outlaws lived in those same forests. The Forest Laws as they existed in the Middle Ages (when we find the earliest written references to Robin Hood's adventures) were extremely harsh and universally hated by the peasants who were forced to abide by them. These laws strictly limited their use of the forest's resources. Nuts, fruit, mushrooms, and wood could be collected at will, but it was illegal to hunt and kill any forest animal; by law, animals belonged to the king or the local baron, and were frequently referred to as "the King's deer" or "the King's boar." Bear in mind that for the peasant class, meat often meant the difference between living and starving to death.

Any man who could successfully defy the Forest Laws would be a folk hero in the eyes of the peasants, who could only sympathize and rejoice in his victories over the authorities. It is easy to see how real stories of narrow escapes from the law, fights with noblemen, and rescues of fellow outlaws, could be combined with already-established stories of Robin, the bountiful God of the Wood. They were likely told and retold, embellished with each retelling, creating the stuff of legend. From these legends, the Robin Hood ballads and mummer's plays were born.

The Robin Hood Play: Make It Your Own

Remember, personalizing a mummer's play script reflects the spirit of an old and honorable folk custom. Humor is an excellent learning tool, and as we noted earlier, these plays' original purpose was to convey the seasons' lessons—the cycle of birth, death, and rebirth—to illiterate villagers. Adding topical humor is part of the fun of this living tradition. Feel free to add private jokes and references unique to your group: the performance will be more meaningful, relevant, and funnier for you and your audience. Traditionally, most of the lines are rhymed couplets, which are easier to memorize than straight text; this was especially true for a nonliterate society, but it is true for us, too.

A few rehearsals are advisable. If possible, gather your cast several weeks early and rehearse four or five times. The goal is twofold: first, to add your own funny references to the script, and second, to give the actors a chance to memorize their lines. (Performing with scripts in hand detracts from the experience for both actors and audience.) On the other hand, do not over-rehearse! Keep it fresh. Another approach is to spring the scripts and costumes on unsuspecting volunteers immediately before the performance, with actors drawing their roles out of a hat. This can bring an interesting spontaneity to the proceedings.

NOTE FOR PAGAN GROUPS

All participants should ground and center before they begin the play, and personally ground any excess energy afterward.

Robin Hood: A Mummer's Play for Summer

Since no historical Robin Hood Play script exists, I drew on traditional mummer's sources and wrote this one myself in 1994. (I had written an earlier version in 1991 for the high-school ritual dance team my mother led, Old Castle Morris and Garland, incorporating more roles and more dance into the plot.) The characters blend traditional mummer's roles with the familiar folk of legend. Alan A Dale takes on the Fool aspect while Friar Tuck embodies much of the Father Yule/Old Man persona. Taking St. George's place as the Hero, and Lord of Summer, is Robin Hood, naturally. Maid Marian, a Renaissance-era addition to the legend, is Robin's lovely Man-Woman bride. The Sheriff of Nottingham provides opposition to Robin, serving the function of the Dark Brother/Holly King/ Lord of Winter. The only break from tradition is the Hobby Horse's expanded role. For once he instigates the action rather than merely observing and commenting upon it. I thought it was about time!

This play is rated PG-13. Small children aren't likely to catch the innuendos, but bigger kids probably will! Have fun, and remember, you are among the few to perform a Robin Hood Play in about four hundred years.

Materials and Preparation: Casting, Costumes, and Props

Each character needs a costume, and some need props. Use these costume descriptions as guides; you may be as simple or as elaborate as you wish.

ALAN A DALE

The Fool can be played by either a man or a woman. Alan should wear either the classic Renaissance-era jester's tunic or smock with the sunburst "Kermit-the-Frog" collar and multi-pointed hat, bright clownlike clothes, or tattered raglike clothes—preferably ones that don't match. He or she may carry a guitar or other stringed instrument, if desired.

FRIAR TUCK

Friar Tuck, too, can be played by either a man or a woman. I suggest a monastic brown belted robe and a large tankard. A very large tankard.

HOBBY HORSE

This role can also be played by either gender. For costuming options, see pages 22–23.

ROBIN HOOD

Robin Hood can be played by either a man or a woman, but see the casting recommendations for the next two roles as well. Robin should wear the classic green tunic and feathered cap, à la Errol Flynn. He will need a sword (the toy wooden type is safest).

MAID MARIAN

The Man-Woman is traditionally played by a man, but in any case should be of the same gender as the actor playing Robin Hood. Marian will need woman's clothes: skirt, blouse, dress, apron, and a wig or hat. Remember, water balloons or water-filled unlubricated condoms stuffed into a very large old bra make good breasts.

SHERIFF OF NOTTINGHAM

This role, too, should be the same gender as the actors playing Robin Hood and Maid Marian, again to keep the play's message from degenerating into a battle of the sexes. The Sheriff is dressed in black and also carries a wooden sword.

Cast of Characters

(in order of appearance)
Alan A Dale
Friar Tuck
Hobby Horse
Robin Hood
Maid Marian
Sheriff of Nottingham

Alan A Dale

Room, make room! Give us room to stand!
And we'll tell you a story of Old England.
In comes I, Alan A Dale,
Teller of this fearsome tale.
We bring you the story of Robin Hood
And his Merry Men, who live in Sherwood.
I hope you enjoy our mummer's play,
So come in, Friar Tuck, without delay!

Friar Tuck

Welcome or welcome not, here I come
Old Friar Tuck to start the fun.
Life in the forest isn't so bad,
There's plenty of hearty food to be had:
Roast deer, fresh fish, strong ale and mince pie,
Now who likes that any better than I?

Hobby Horse

Me-ee-ee-ee!

Alan A Dale

Come in, Hobby Horse, come in!

Robin Hood

In comes I, Robin Hood, old England's pride.

And this is Maid Marian, my beautiful bride.

I rob from the rich and give to the poor;

What else is a people's champion for?

When it comes to fighting I'm the best there is.

I can beat any man with a staff, a bow or . . .

Sheriff of Nottingham

A kiss.

Robin Hood

See here, Sheriff, I am Robin Hood.

Insults like that just aren't very good.

Sheriff of Nottingham

Robin, I want you to listen and know

Why it is that I hate you so.

I raise the taxes, you steal them from me.

The things I sell to the poor you give free.

I am feared like the dark of night,

While you are worshiped like the sun's true light.

You are so much loved by the lower class

That you're really becoming a pain in my . . . neck.

I think you're trying to ruin my life.

You even made my beloved Marian your wife!

Maid Marian

I'd rather have died than marry you!

Robin Hood

Hush, my darling. What can I say?
Marian loves me, she's Queen of the May.

The Sheriff grabs Marian away from Robin and holds her captive with the edge of his sword across her torso.

Sheriff of Nottingham

Nobody move—or else she dies.
She'll bleed to death before your eyes!
Helpless, aren't you, without your bow?
So who is going to save her now?

The Hobby Horse runs up behind the Sheriff and knocks him over.

Hobby Horse

Me-ee-ee-ee!

Maid Marian runs to the protection of Friar Tuck.

Robin Hood

I may not have my bow, but I still have my sword
Let us see if you're as good as your word!

Sheriff of Nottingham

A battle, a battle then, I cry!
To see who on this ground shall lie.

Robin Hood

You want a battle? Then a battle you shall have!
You have threatened my Lady, and my love.

They fight. Robin is mortally wounded.

Robin Hood

My blood is spilled by this cruel man,
I die for love, and for the land.

He dies gloriously. Marian throws herself on the body.

Maid Marian

Robin!

Friar Tuck

Oh, cruel Sheriff, what have you done?
You have killed our belov-ed one.

Sheriff of Nottingham

Oops?

Hobby Horse

Neigh!

Friar Tuck

The death of Robin Hood is very tragic,
He must be resurrected with magic.

Alan A Dale is wandering around and trips over the body.

Alan A Dale

Rough ground!

Maid Marian

Father, I beg you, let me try.
The bond 'twixt Robin and me cannot die.
Hobby, help me revive my lord!

The Hobby Horse goes to Marian and whispers in her ear.

Maid Marian

Uh, okay.

Wake up, Robin, and I will make you a shirt of silk, softer than down and
as white as snow!

*All lean forward in great anticipation, but nothing happens. The Hobby Horse again
whispers in Marian's ear.*

Maid Marian

You think so?

Wake up, Robin, and I will give you gold, jewels, treasure, riches beyond
your imagination!

*Again, all lean forward in great anticipation, but nothing happens. The Hobby Horse
again whispers in Marian's ear.*

Maid Marian

Are you sure?

Hobby Horse

Aaaaay!

Maid Marian

Wake up, Robin, and I will give you the key to my garden of earthly
delights, that you will always have sweet nectar to drink and fragrant
blossoms to touch.

Robin leaps up instantly. All cheer.

Robin Hood

Good morrow, gentles all—
A-sleeping I have been.
And such a sleep I've had,

The like was never seen!
I was knocked out of my seven senses
And into seventeen!

He spies the Sheriff trying to sneak away.

But now I'm awake, the fight I'll resume,
And quickly send THEE to thy doom!

They fight, and the Sheriff is quickly disarmed.

Sheriff of Nottingham
Oh, pits.

Robin Hood
Begone from us, Sheriff of Nottingham!
We've seen who is the better man.
Please don't make me fight you again,
For the sun is strong, and I'm certain to win!

Sheriff of Nottingham
I will have my time, my brother.

Robin Hood
I know, my brother, but not today.

The Sheriff stomps off like a little kid having a tantrum.

Maid Marian
My hero!

They reunite enthusiastically.

Alan A Dale
My hero!

He does to Friar Tuck whatever Marian did to Robin.

When they are finished, Robin addresses the audience, still holding Marian's hand.

Robin Hood
Good people, listen to what I say:
We learned an important lesson today.
Winter's cold and summer's sun,
Darkness and Light are all part of the One.
Only when we know this well
Can we be One within ourselves.
Over pain and laughter, over death and rebirth,
Love is the strongest force on Earth.

Friar Tuck
Now let the music play, and make the forest ring!
A sip of English ale will make us laugh and sing!
But the Sheriff's gold in our pockets is a much better thing!
With cheese in the larder and our bellies full of beer,
We thank you, and wish you all much cheer!

All collect money from the audience while singing an appropriate song, such as those on the following pages.

Rosebud in June

Traditionally, June was the month for sheep-shearing in England. There are many songs on the subject, which is not surprising: sheep products frequently made the difference between surviving the winter—or not. In addition to wool, sheep offered mutton and tallow (fat used in making medicines, waterproofing, and candlemaking).

1. It's a rosebud in June and the violets in full bloom,
   And the songbird singing love songs on each spray.

   Chorus:
   > We'll pipe and we'll sing, love, we'll dance in a ring, love.
   > When each lad takes his lass all on the green grass.
   > And it's all to plough
   > Where the fat oxen graze low,
   > And the lads and the lasses do sheep-shearing go.

2. When we have all sheared our jolly, jolly sheep,
   What jot can be greater than to talk of their increase?

   Chorus

3. For their flesh it is good. It's the best of all food.
   And their wool it will clothe us and keep our backs from the cold.

   Chorus

4. Here's the ewes and the lambs. Here's the horns and the rams.
   And the fat withers, too. They will make a fine show.

   Chorus

Wild Mountain Thyme

Even though this song is not considered traditional, as it was written in 1957 by Frank McPeake of Belfast, it expresses the old and beautiful sentiment of summer love. Depending on the sexual orientation of the singer(s), you can use either "lassie" or "laddie" or both.

1. O, the summer time is coming,
   And the trees are sweetly blooming,
   And the wild mountain thyme
   Grows around the purple heather.
   Will you go, lassie, go?

   Chorus:
   And we'll all go together
   To pull wild mountain thyme,
   All around the blooming heather,
   Will you go, lassie, go?

2. I will build my love a bower
   By yon clear crystal fountain.
   And on it I will pile
   All the flowers of our mountain.
   Will you go, lassie, go?

   Chorus

3. If my true love she is gone
   I would surely find no other
   To pull wild mountain thyme
   All around the purple heather.
   Will you go, lassie, go?

   Chorus

Collected by Peter Kennedy from the McPeake family of Belfast, Ireland.

The Queen Among the Heather

Frank McPeake may have used this traditional piece as inspiration for *Wild Mountain Thyme*.

1. For it's up a wide and a lonely glen
   It was shed by many's a lofty mountain,
   It being onto the busy haunts of men,
   It being the first day that I went out a-hunting.

2. For it's been to me a happy day
   The day I spied my rovin' fancy.
   She was herding her yowes over the knows
   And down amongst the curlin' heather.

3. For her coat was white and her gown was green,
   Her body it being long and slender,
   With her cast-down looks and her well-fared face
   It has oft-times made my heart to wander.

4. For it's I've been to balls where they were bust-eye and braw.
   And it's I've been to London and Balquither.
   And the bonniest lass that e'er I saw
   She was kilted and barefoot amongst the heather.

5. Says I, "My lass, will you come with me
   And sleep with me in a bed of feathers?
   I'll gie you silks and scarlets that will make you shine
   If you'll be my queen among the heather."

6. She said, "My lad, your offer's fair
   And I think you're all for laughter.
   For it's you being the son of a high squire man
   And me but a poor humble shepherd's daughter."

7. But it's her I sought and her I got
   And with her I intend to be contented.
   Fare you well, fare you well to your heathery hill.
   Fare you well, fare you well, my song is ended.

New Mown Hay

This is one of many songs in the English folk tradition that celebrate the cycle of planting and harvesting—understandably, since all life, human and animal, depended on a successful harvest.

Chorus: I like to rise when the sun she ri - ses Ear - ly in the morn - ing.

I like to hear those small birds sing-ing Mer-ri-ly up-on the lay - lums. And hu -

rah for the life of a coun-try boy To go ramb-lin' in the new mown hay.   In the

win-ter when the sky is gray We edge and we ditch our time a-way. But in the

sum - mer when the sun shines gay We go ramb-lin' in the new mown hay.

Chorus:
> I like to rise when the sun she rises
> Early in the morning.
> I like to hear those small birds singing
> Merrily upon the laylums.[2]
> And hurrah for the life of a country boy
> To go ramblin' in the new-mown hay.

1. In the winter when the sky is gray,
    We edge and we ditch our time away.
    But in the summer when the sun shines gay
    We go ramblin' in the new-mown hay.

    Chorus

2. In the spring we sow, at the harvest mow
    And that's how the seasons 'round they go.
    But of all the life if choose I may
    Would be ramblin' in the new-mown hay.

    Chorus

---

2 "Lay" is an Elizabethan word for "song." "Lum" is a nonsense syllable common to English folk songs to help the words fit the music.

The Bold Pedlar and Robin Hood

Of the countless ballads and variants about Robin Hood and his Merry Men, this song seems to be one of the rare ones with a singable tune and fewer than fifty verses.

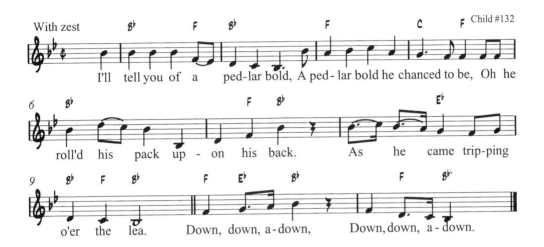

1. I'll tell you of a pedlar bold,
   A pedlar bold he chanced to be.
   Oh he roll'd his pack upon his back
   As he came a-tripping o'er the lea.

   Chorus:
   > Down, down, a-down,
   > Down, down, a-down.

2. "What have you got, you pedlar trim?
   What have you got, pray tell to me?"
   "It's seven suits of the gay green silk,
   Besides my bow-strings, two or three."

   Chorus

3. "If you've seven suits of the gay green silk,
   Besides your bow-strings, two or three;

Upon my word," said Little John,
"One half of them belong to me."

Chorus

4. The pedlar then took off his pack
   And laid it down most manfully.
   Saying, "The man that can drive me two feet from this,
   The pack and all I will give to thee."

Chorus

5. Then Robin Hood, he drew his sword,
   The noble pedlar held his hand.
   They swaggered swords 'til the blood did drop,
   Saying, "Noble pedlar, stay your hand."

Chorus

6. "What is your name, you pedlar trim?
   What is your name, pray tell to me?"
   "Not one bit of it—my name—you'll get
   'Til both of yours you tell to me."

Chorus

7. "My name is Bold Robin Hood,
   The other, Little John so free.
   And now it lies within your breast
   To tell us what your name can be."

Chorus

8. "My name is Bold Gammon gay,
   And I come far beyond the sea;
   For killing a man in my father's court,
   I was banished from my own country."

Chorus

9. "Your name it is Bold Gammon gay,
   And you come far beyond the sea.
   And if we are two sisters' sons,
   What nearer kindred need we be?"

   Chorus

AUTUMN

One slightly foggy September evening in 1971, my parents and I joined a group of onlookers on the library steps of Berea College in central Kentucky. The school's folk dance troupe was performing a variety of dances from the United States and England, and as an eight-year-old I was delighted to attend. We faced a large grass-covered square punctuated with ancient oak and maple trees, which set the mood for the village green and county fair settings we anticipated in the dances to come.

But these friendly images were transformed into a forest primeval when, from the opposite end of the slowly darkening square, a lone musician appeared, playing a wooden recorder. As if in response to his haunting melody, six masked dancers, each garbed in a green tabard and holding a rack of stag antlers to his forehead, stepped out from behind the trees. They were followed in procession by a Man-Woman, a Hobby Horse, a young green-clad boy carrying a bow and arrow, and a Fool. The dancers wove single file through the trees to the performance area, then formed a small circle that fell into two facing lines.

The lines advanced toward each other and retreated, each Stag Dancer clashing horns with the one opposite, the Character Dancers bowing to each other as they advanced again and again. The audience was silent with awe; the dancers' feet were silent on the grass. The only sounds were the mournful piper and the primal clash of the antlers. Eventually they re-formed into a single file and, again following the musician, wove back through the trees . . . and vanished into the evening mist as if they had never been there.

That was the night I first met the Horned God face to face . . .

The Abbots Bromley Horn Dance

This dance is an oddity in the English ritual tradition: it is the only dance originating in the British Isles in which some participants dress as animals. Honoring the hunt and the deer of the forest, this stately, otherworldly ritual is performed only in Autumn and Midwinter: a four-month period beginning on the first Monday after September 4 and ending on Twelfth Night, January 6.

Today it is performed in both England and the United States—with some clear differences. At Abbots Bromley Manor in England, the site of the original team, the dancers are out all day, passing the hat to raise money for various church charities, and using any tune that the accompanying musician happens to know—these have been known to include "Yankee Doodle" and current pop songs.

In America, the dance is almost always part of a full day or evening's performance of ritual dance and song. Most notably, it is often included in the pageants staged by Revels, Inc. These companies' productions are filled with folk song and dance and are staged annually in cities nationwide. And although witnessing the performance of the Horn Dance is said to bring luck in the coming year, funds are never collected from U.S. audiences to guarantee that luck.

American teams all use the same tune, printed here. This slow, mournful melody probably contributes to the sense of almost trance-like mystical awe reported by nearly every dancer. This is also the only English ritual dance tradition in America where the dancers sometimes deliberately dress to maintain their sacred anonymity by wearing masks or hoods.

The dance has been performed at Abbots Bromley Manor every Autumn for centuries. Other teams have come to it only within the last four or five generations, drawn to it by its unique nature, and also by the publicity generated by the early folklorists who rediscovered it around the turn of the twentieth century. Unfortunately, there is no way to tell for sure just how old this dance is. The performers move primarily in single file, and dance historians and cultural anthropologists are quick to point out that single file is the oldest dance pattern there is, and one that is still used exclusively by some tribal peoples. (Circle dances, square dances, and two-line forms such as reels and contras are much more recent.)

The horns used today by the Abbots Bromley Manor team weigh between sixteen and twenty-five pounds and come from a particular species of reindeer that, interestingly, was never native to the British Isles. Recent carbon dating shows that at least one of the horns in this collection came from an animal killed in the year 1065, plus or minus eighty years.

Some scholars have tried to assign possible Druidic origins to this dance because of the deer symbolism and the noteworthy antiquity of the original antlers. The very nature of the Horn Dance itself suggests a strong connection with hunt magic and possibly fertility magic as well. The horn-clashing movement easily evokes images of young stags fighting for the favors of a particular doe.

As with the morris dance, we find our four extra characters in silent attendance—roles we already know through the mummer's plays. It is difficult to clearly define the roles of the four Character Dancers that follow the Stag Dancers. The Man-Woman points to the fertility aspect of the dance, and the Hobby Horse, as we have seen, signifies the journey of the soul from life to death. Often the boy carrying the bow and arrow is referred to as the Hunter, and the Fool brings up the rear. Perhaps, as in the mummer's play, the Fool is there to witness, to make the proceedings sacred with his presence.

Some Practical Matters for Pagan and Non-Pagan Groups

WOMEN DANCERS

Should women perform in the Abbots Bromley Horn Dance? Opinions vary in the folk dance community. Many "traditional" (that is, all-male) ritual dance teams feel that it is a surviving form of hunt magic and women should not participate—any more than men should partake in childbearing rituals. However, some men's teams concede that it's fine for women to dance the character positions—Man-Woman, Hobby Horse, Boy, or Fool. Mixed teams (both sexes) generally see no problem with both genders performing the dance. In fact, many teams have few enough members that no other option is available if they wish to do the Horn Dance at all.

As for me, I agree that the dance is uniquely men's magic. I have performed with mixed morris teams, danced longsword at dance camps, and directed and performed in mummer's plays for large audiences—but I have never done the Abbots Bromley Horn Dance outside of my own Pagan group's Fall Equinox celebration, and I have no plans to change that. Frankly, as a woman I would feel extremely uncomfortable doing so. But for a women's or mixed-gender group, if the only alternative is to avoid the dance altogether, then I would rather see women perform it. Whether you're a dancer or in the audience, it's a powerful ritual experience that shouldn't be missed.

TRANCE STATES

For years, dancers have reported slipping into a light trance during the Horn Dance. Whether this is because of the mesmerizing tune, the simplicity of the figures, a personal connection to the Divine, or all of the above, is difficult to say. Even the most cynical agnostic has been known to admit that "something was different" during the dance. This possible trance state is something the dance leader, or Head Stag, needs to be aware of.

FOR PAGAN GROUPS IN PARTICULAR

Because this dance is not strenuous and involves no sharp implements, I feel that ritual garb, including skyclad, is acceptable attire for the Stag Dancers. All participants should ground and center before they begin dancing, and should personally ground any excess energy afterward—for this dance more than any of the other activities in this book.

Abbots Bromley Horn Dance: Instructions

In this stately, mysterious dance, several Stag Dancers and four Character Dancers form a line, led by Stag 1, that snakes to the performance area. The performers circle in a looping pattern, reversing the direction of the circle, dance briefly in two rows, then return to the line formation to repeat the dance.

Materials and Preparation

MASKS OR FACE DISGUISES

The traditional method of blackening the face with burnt cork works well. The cork is easily removed with soap or facial cream and water, and is less sticky and itchy than camouflage paint or stage makeup. Some teams have made plain green or brown fabric masks that completely cover the head and face except for eyeholes. A full cowl or hood pulled up over the head would work too.

ANTLERS

Each Stag Dancer needs a pair of deer antlers linked with part of the skull bone. Unless enough people in your group already own such antlers, perhaps as altar pieces, and are willing to lend them, you will have to acquire them yourself. This can be difficult—and

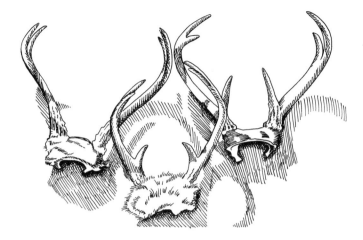

These are good antlers for the Abbots Bromley Horn Dance.

a little ghoulish. Unfortunately, using antlers from still-living animals is very unlikely. Even though deer shed their antlers every year, they generally fall off separately, and in any case are quickly damaged by insects.

If you're a hunter who lives in a rural area with a deer season, you're in luck, of course. Or if you know any hunters, tell them what you're looking for. Or talk to the nice people at your local deer check-in station, both before and during the season: tell them you'll take any sets of antlers the hunters leave behind. Then go there on weekends and wait for them to arrive. Expect some racks to be puny, as hunters like to keep the bigger ones themselves. And be prepared to accept an entire deer head. When my parents were acquiring eight sets of antlers for a teen dance team, one Sunday morning they found an entire deer head in a black plastic trash bag on their front porch! If that happens to you, don't panic. Your local taxidermist or butcher can remove the parts you don't want. Another source: deer that have died by the road after being hit by a car. If you see one and the antlers look usable, try to take the whole carcass with you right away; it may not be there later. (You might keep a plastic tarp in your trunk just in case.) Report the carcass to the check-in station if it's open, or to the police. Many states have strict laws that penalize anyone caught with a dead deer out of season, or with no hunting license. Again, enlist a taxidermist or a butcher to help.

These methods require a strong stomach and an equally strong sense of humor. If you don't happen to have both, or you're a city dweller, there are alternatives. Look for antlers in flea markets and yard sales: you might find great-uncle Chester's prize trophy that his heirs are eager to dispose of. Look in junk shops and curio shops. Check the Internet—not only eBay, but websites that deal in animal hides and other products. (Type "deer antlers for sale" into your search engine.) Consider any contacts you may have in the Native American community; if you *politely* explain why you need the antlers, they might have what you're looking for.

Before use in any sacred setting—including the Horn Dance—antlers should be cared for properly, especially if they were acquired from hunters or roadside mishaps. A basic ritual can be found in appendix C, "Cleansing and Releasing Rite." It is wise to perform this ritual on any antlers, regardless of source, unless you can verify personally that the animal was humanely euthanized.

COSTUMES AND PROPS FOR CHARACTER DANCERS

The *Man-Woman* wears women's clothes—skirt, blouse, apron—and traditionally carries a large soup or tea ladle or a parasol. Add a wig or hat unless the gentleman playing her has styleable long hair. The *Hobby Horse*—or Sheep, Mule, Camel—should be the Renaissance-era horse and rider described on page 22, since this dancer needs good vision. (The two-person horse or the primitive horse-head and fabric drape are likely to crash into other dancers or even wander off without knowing it.) The *Boy or Hunter* carries a small bow and arrow (which need not be real) and usually wears a green tunic and Robin Hood-like cap. For the *Fool,* the classic jester's tunic with the sunburst "Kermit the Frog" collar and pointed hat is great, but any bright clownlike garb or tattered raglike clothes will do, preferably ones that don't quite match. Traditionally, the Fool carries a triangle, that wonderful instrument from elementary school music class that adults never take seriously. If your Fool decides to carry one, it should be struck at odd, random moments in the dance, unrelated to the beat. (Remember: when striking the triangle, less is more.)

Music

The music is in 6/8 time, with three sections: A, B, and C, each with eight bars. The tune shown here is used universally by American morris or sword teams for this dance, and by some English teams that have incorporated it into their repertoire. This tune's power is strongest when it is played by a solo instrument—a fiddle, pennywhistle, recorder, or maybe even a concertina; in fact, every team I have seen perform this dance has made that choice. So no accompanying chords are shown here.

The Step

The step is stately and dignified, in time with the music. As in the longsword dance, other than softly spoken instructions from the Head Stag (Stag 1), the performers are silent.

Preliminaries

- Ten people traditionally do this dance: six Stag Dancers and four Character Dancers. (Add or subtract Stags if your group is larger or smaller—but keep an *even number* of Stags; four is the minimum.)

- Assuming ten dancers: count off one through ten, starting with the six Stags. Put your best dancers in the 1 and 4 slots. They have to think!

- Stags, hold your antlers at forehead level in both hands with palms out, elbows at about ear level. You will hold them this way throughout—which is more tiring than it looks, even with small antlers that seem light at first.

Dance Instructions

1. *Circle up.* All dancers stand in single file behind the Head Stag (Stag 1). After the six stags come the Man-Woman, the Hobby Horse, the Boy (or Hunter) and the Fool in that order. When the music starts, the dancers follow Stag 1 to their performance location, say, the group's ritual room or outdoor ritual space. Stag 1 leads the others in a random pattern until the A music begins again, then leads all dancers into a large moving circle. (The direction is not important, but I recommend to the right, or counterclockwise.) All circle until the B music begins, when they will begin the next figure.

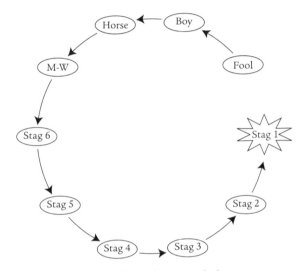

Circle up: All circle counterclockwise.

2. *One leads off.* When the B music starts, Stag 1 breaks the circle by turning into it, briefly exchanging a bow with Stag 2, then leading the line of dance into a small loop-the-loop. Stags 1 and 2 pass between Stags 3 and 4, who now pivot and continue in the loop that is being formed. All other dancers follow in this formation:

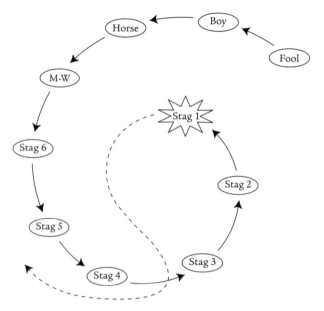

Stag 1 breaks the circle and leads the line in a small loop, then away.

(Note: As soon as Stag 3 passes through the spot where the space between Stags 3 and 4 used to be, Stag 4 falls into place behind Stag 3, leading the rest of the dancers along the looping line. Stag 4's precision and timing here are key.) As the other dancers retrace the looping line, Stag 1 leads the line away in any direction, the goal being to create a circle going the opposite way (see next figure). Here, Stag 1 is shown taking a doubling-back route.

3. *Circle in the opposite direction.* Stag 1 leads the doubled-back line into a circle turning clockwise (opposite from the original).

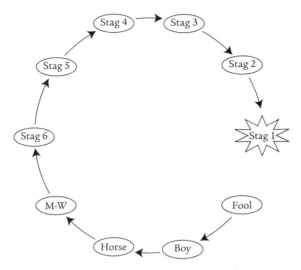

The line now forms a circle moving clockwise.

Once the circle is re-formed, the dancers prepare for the "all together."

4. *All together.* After the circle is reestablished and about two bars before the C music starts, the dancers form two lines and prepare for the next figure.

5. *Advance-meet-retire.* When the C music begins, all dancers take three steps forward in their lines, starting on the left foot. On the fourth beat, all Stags raise their right leg forward and up and *lightly* clash horns while the Character Dancers bow slightly to each other. This moment has the feel of a challenge, even in the bow: a martial-arts style bow would be appropriate—from the hips, with the dancers keeping eye contact. All dancers then retire to place (take four small steps backwards), repeat the advance-meet-retire, then prepare for the cross-over.

6. *Cross-over and repeat.* In the second phrase of the C music (after the second advance-meet-retire), dancers step forward on the left foot again, but this time they cross over and change sides with the dancer opposite, passing *right* shoulders. Then they repeat the advance-meet-retire and cross-over figures, starting on the *right* foot this time, ending with all dancers crossing back to their original sides. The dance is ready to begin again when the A music resumes.

7. *Form the line.* When the A music starts, Stag 1 dances forward, followed by the rest of the dancers, turning *away* from the two lines by turning over his or her left shoulder:

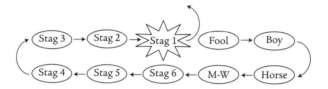

All dancers process to a new location, or circle in the same location. When the B music starts again, Stag 1 again leads the "one leads off" figure. The dance has started again.

The John Barleycorn Play

In the mummer's plays in this book's Winter section, St. George, either in his role as the Sacred King or as the Solar Hero, died and was brought back to life. In the Spring Wooing Play, the Old Man, symbolizing the Lady's old lover, made way for the new lover, the Fool. In Summer, the ever-popular Jack-of-the-Green in his Robin Hood persona died in combat and was revived. Now, at the Harvest time of year, our hero in the mummer's play is John Barleycorn, symbolizing the God of Vegetation who ripens and dies every Fall.

Unlike her aging lover-Goddess counterpart in the Wooing Play, the Old Woman in this play takes on many of the magical aspects of Grandfather Yule. She is the Crone, and all ancient powers and wisdom are at her command. The Fool and the Doctor have more opportunity to interact in this play. Considering the common origin of both characters, this has the potential to be very, very funny.

In creating this play, I relied heavily on the mummer's play text presented in Richard Chase's book *Grandfather Tales*. Chase himself directed a nearly identical version at a folk dance festival in Kentucky on New Year's Eve in 1967. And like Chase, I have also drawn upon the original folk song for inspiration. (See songs at the end of this section.)

Materials and Preparation: Casting, Costumes, and Props

Again, each character needs a costume or some form of disguise, and some need props. A few of the costumes needed for this particular play are different from the ones used elsewhere in the book, as the characters are unique.

JACK FINNEY

The Fool can be played by either a man or a woman. As in the other plays, he wears either the classic Renaissance-era jester's tunic with the sunburst "Kermit the Frog" collar and pointed hat, bright clownlike clothes, or tattered raglike clothes—preferably ones that don't quite match. He or she also needs a broom.

OLD WOMAN

Whether played by a man or a woman, she is a Crone figure and should be played as such, dressed in a black robe and shawl, and carrying a tall staff. She doesn't need the child or the frying pan, this time.

MISS MOLLY MCGEE

The Man-Woman really should be played by a man, preferably one with a beard. Remember, it's traditional and it's funny. Like her sisters Griselda the Fair (Winter), Dame Jane (Spring), and Maid Marian (Summer), the Man-Woman will need woman's clothes: skirt, blouse, apron, and a wig or hat—unless the gentleman playing her has long, styleable hair. Again, water balloons stuffed into a very large old bra make excellent breasts, and unlubridated condoms make good, durable water balloons.

JOHN BARLEYCORN

Barleycorn can be played by a man or a woman, preferably a youthful one either way. To underscore his vegetative aspects, I suggest he wear a green robe (perhaps he can borrow Father Yule's or Robin Hood's). For most of the play, Barleycorn is an old man with a false white beard and a cane. But when the Old Woman speaks her incantation, Barleycorn is suddenly made young. The other characters, clustering around him, can pull off the beard, hiding it and the cane. Another option is to cast two people as John Barleycorn: an adult and a child. The child steps into the knot of characters during the incantation and the adult John sneaks away. Ideally, the child can read or memorize John's final lines; otherwise, someone else can speak them.

MAN 1, 2, AND 3

These can be male or female, or a mix, and should dress alike. Again, I suggest blue or black jeans, white shirts, and dark vests for either sex. They will need swords, ideally longsword dance swords or wooden swords, but any dull-edged swords work fine.

DOCTOR BALL

Doctor Ball can be played by either a man or a woman. As in the other plays, the Doctor can wear either a white lab coat over regular clothes, surgical scrubs, or a golfing costume: knickers, sweater vest, tweed golf cap. Again, the Doctor will need a medical bag with an empty or water-filled liquor bottle and anything else the imagination can concoct. More suggestions: a stuffed cat (for a "cat" scan), strange and obscure kitchen utensils, a hand-bellows, magician's flowers, whole raw potatoes, a rubber chicken, and an old wig.

HOBBY HORSE

The Hobby Horse can be played by either a man or a woman. The costume can either be the primitive or Renaissance-era versions described in the Winter section. (See illustrations on page 23.)

Cast of Characters
(in order of appearance)
Jack Finney
Old Woman
Miss Molly McGee
John Barleycorn
Man 1
Man 2
Man 3
Doctor Ball
Hobby Horse

Jack Finney
Open the door and let us in!
We hope your favor we shall win.
Whether we stand or whether we fall,
We'll do our best to please you all.

Room! Room! Make room! Make room!
Make room to let us play!
We'll show you some activity
Upon this holiday.

I'm Jack Finney, with a broom before
To sweep the dirt behind the door.
We come here to wish you cheer,
Money in your pockets and your bellies full of beer.

Come in, Old Woman!

Old Woman

In comes I, Old Woman, hard times or not,
I know Old Woman will never be forgot.
The Lady bless your hearth and fold,
Shut out the wolf and keep out the cold.

Jack Finney

Come in, Miss Molly McGee!

Molly McGee

In comes I, Miss Molly McGee!
So bee-u-tiful I be
That every man around this place
Must now be kissed by me.

She attempts to make this happen.

Jack Finney

And now our hero, he shall come.
It is for him this play is done.
Come in, John Barleycorn.

John Barleycorn

In comes I, John Barleycorn, the best in the land.
I'll stand and I'll fall
For the sake of you all.

Jack Finney

I've brought some gallant men with me
To show you great activity.
Activity of youth from an ancient age,
Activity like you've never seen on stage.
These three men come out of the West,
Let them do what they do best.

Three men enter with swords. With ritualized movements, which greatly interest Barleycorn, they create a triangle out of their swords and place it around his neck.

Jack Finney
Now, John Barleycorn, you must die.

John Barleycorn
Me? Die? How must I die?

Jack Finney
We are going to cut off your head.

John Barleycorn
Well! I never had my head cut off before in all my life,
that I can remember . . .

Jack Finney
Stand, John Barleycorn! You must be cut down!

John Barleycorn
Very well then, if I must die I will die,
With my face toward the sun, for all of you.

The men draw their swords, and Barleycorn falls.

Molly McGee
Horrible, terrible! See what they've done!
They've killed our own belov-ed one!

Old Woman
They've cut him down like the evening sun!

Jack Finney trips over John Barleycorn.

Jack Finney

Rough ground!

Man 1

What's going on here?

Jack Finney

Dead man! Look!

Man 1

Those two other fellows did it! Hey, you villains!
You cut-throats! Come back here and clear yourselves!

Man 2

I'm sure it's none of I that did this bloody act.
It's him that follows me that did it for a fact.

Man 2 points to Man 3.

Man 3

The Fool here did this deed and lays it off on me.
Come, rapscallion! Get a sword, and I will fight with thee!

Jack Finney

Peace! If you want to fight, join the National Guard.

Man 2

We must call a doctor! Doctor, oh Doctor!

Jack Finney

Is there a doctor in the house? Doctor? Doctor?

All

Is there a doctor to be found,
Can cure this deep and deadly wound?
Doctor, doctor play thy part,
Barleycorn's wounded in the heart.

Jack Finney

Here comes a doctor, true and good.
And with his hand he'll stanch the blood.

Doctor enters with Hobby Horse.

Doctor Ball

In comes I, Old Doctor Ball.
Cure none, kill them all!
Hold my horse, Jack Finney.

Jack Finney

Will he bite?

Doctor Ball

No.

Jack Finney

Will he kick?

Doctor Ball

No.

Jack Finney

Take two to hold him?

Doctor Ball

NO!

Jack Finney

Then hold him yourself, then.

Doctor Ball

What's that, you saucy young rascal?

Jack Finney

I've got him, sir.

Doctor Ball

Mm-m! Now, boys, what's the trouble here?

Old Woman

Man's dead. Head's been cut off.

Doctor Ball

Mm-m. How long has he been dead?

Man 3

Just a minute ago . . .

Man 1

Early this morning . . .

Man 2

Day before yesterday . . .

Man 3

About two weeks ago!

Doctor Ball

Two weeks! You don't need a doctor, you need an undertaker!

(to Hobby Horse)

Let's go, Ned.

Jack Finney

No, no! You must try to cure him, Doctor. Please!

Old Woman

Wait a minute!

What's your fee, Doctor?

Doctor Ball

Eleven guineas, nineteen shillings, eleven pence, three farthings,

a peck of gingerbread for me, a loaf of oats for my horse.

Hobby Horse is delighted.

Old Woman

That's too much! Can't you knock it down a little, Doctor?

Doctor Ball

Well, I'll knock off five

If I can't cure this man alive . . . and the oats.

Hobby Horse is crestfallen. Maybe kicks Doctor.

Jack Finney

Do you think you can cure him, Doctor?

Doctor Ball

Hold up his head.

With what's in this bottle, I can raise the dead!

Jack Finney

What did you say was in this bottle, Doctor?

Doctor Ball

One drop of tincture of nim-nam,

One teaspoon of essence of nim-nam,

Three quarts of nim-nam itself,

One jigger of good Irish whisky,

One ounce of brains from a sawhorse,

One pound of marrow out of a stool leg,

All stirred with a green frog's feather.

Man 1

Sounds good to me!

He tries to get the bottle. The other two men help him, and may or may not succeed.

Old Woman

What can you cure?

Doctor Ball

All diseases, coughs and sneezes,

And anything else my physic pleases.

The itch, the stitch, the palsy, the gout.

Pains in the belly and pains all about.

If a man has nineteen devils in him, I can get twenty out.

Molly McGee

I'm convinced, Sweetcheeks!

Old Woman

How came you to be a doctor?

Doctor Ball

By my travels.
I've traveled to Italy, Sicily, France, and Spain
Germany, Iceland, and back again.
I've seen houses topped with pancakes high,
Streets lined with plum pudding
And little pigs running around with knives and forks
in their back crying, "Who'll eat me? Who'll eat me?"
Well, enough said.
Let's raise this poor man from the dead.

Doctor Ball performs some silly business trying to cure Barleycorn, unsuccessfully.

Jack Finney

Well, Doctor. Looks like you've made a bobble of it.
Stand back, and let's see what I can do for this man.

Molly McGee elbows him out of the way.

Molly McGee

Do for a man? Let ME have a try . . .
Bushel of wheat, bushel of rye
This poor old man he had to die.
Bushel of corn, bushel of clover
When he died . . . he died all over!

Old Woman

ENOUGH!

All except Old Woman huddle around Barleycorn and help remove beard, or replace him with Young John as planned.

Now rise, thou youth of jollity
And flourish for this company.

You shall have no beard, your hair be thick,
Your body pliant as a hazel stick.
John Barleycorn, you're in a trance,
Arise young man, and join our dance!

All lift John Barleycorn, now a young man, to his feet.

John Barleycorn

Good morning gentlemen, a-sleeping I have been
And such a sleep I've had, the like was never seen.
But now I'm awake, and this news I bring:
The Circle of Life is a wondrous thing!
Old age is but a doorway into new youth.
My friends, I tell you the absolute truth.

Old Woman

Now let the music play, the harvest we will bring!
A sip of English ale will make us laugh and sing,
But money in our pockets is a much better thing!
With cheese in the larder and our bellies full of beer,
We thank you, and wish you all much cheer!

All collect money from the audience while singing "John Barleycorn" —see page 175.

All Soul's Night and the Soul-Cakers' Play

Another autumnal mummer's play, this one is closely associated with the custom of Souling, a predecessor to the American Halloween trick-or-treat. The Souling or Soul-Cakers' Play is performed on Samhain Night in Cheshire and Shropshire, England. On this night, also called All Soul's Night, children traditionally went from house to house begging soul-cakes, sometimes called dole-cakes or Saumas-cakes. Depending on village custom, these were small fruitcakes, sweet buns, or loaves of wheat bread. The children often sang some version of the souling song (see page 181).

In Celtic tradition, the souls of the departed return to visit their families at Samhain, when the veil separating the realms of the living and the dead is thinnest. In ancient times, the collected cakes, as well as drink and tobacco, were left on the family dining table overnight as an offering to the dead. The Soul-Cakers' Play was most likely another way to collect the cakes, or at least the money to buy them, at the New Year, which was reckoned in the Celtic year as Samhain.

Once again, in this play we see St. George, called King George, and his age-old rival the Turkish Champion, battle to the death in a Hero-Combat Play. In the Winter Play, the Turkish Knight defeats St. George, who is brought back to life again as the embodiment of the new sun. This time King George slays the Turkish Champion, who is brought back to life as the embodiment of the Darkness which is still to come.

Another unique feature of this play: the Doctor finally manages to cure the dead man!

This play is based on a script that was collected in Frodsham, England sometime around 1900. I tightened up the plot somewhat, but the lines and characters are basically unchanged from the original. Be aware—these old lines are somewhat politically incorrect.

Materials and Preparation: Casting, Costumes, and Props

Once again, each character needs a costume or some form of disguise, and some need props.

THE FOOL

As always, the Fool can be played by either a man or a woman, wearing clothing similar to his brother Fools throughout this book. He also needs a broom.

KING GEORGE

King George can be played by either a man or a woman, wearing kingly robes and a crown and carrying a sword.

TURKISH CHAMPION

This role can be played by either a man or a woman, but the same gender as the actor playing King George. He should dress similarly to the Turkish Knight in the Hero-Combat Play (page 35): a belted ankle-length tabard or robe, and a Christmas-pageant-type shepherd's headdress.

OLD WOMAN

Whether played by a man or a woman, she is a Crone-figure and should be played as such. Ideally she should be dressed in a black robe and shawl. She can keep the frying pan, or have some other symbol of her "office"—a cauldron, some bones, etc.

DOCTOR BROWN

Doctor Brown can be played by either a man or a woman, and can dress like his fellow medical men (see page 24). He carries a medical bag with two empty or water-filled liquor bottles and anything else the imagination can concoct. Suggestions: condoms, cell phone, bubble wand, yo-yo, apple, seltzer bottle, loud horn.

Cast of Characters

(in order of appearance)
Fool
King George
Turkish Champion
Old Woman
Doctor Brown

Fool

Open the doors.
Open the doors and let us in.
We have your favour for to win,
Whether we stand, sit, or fall,
We'll do our best to please you all.
Room, room, gallant room do I require,
Step in, King George, and show thy face like fire.

King George

In comes I, King George,
From whom all England sprang.
Many a famous battle I have fought
And made the tyrant tremble on his throne.
Many a long year in close keep have I been
Kept out of that in a prison,
Left out of that in a rock of stone
From whence I made my grievous moan.
I once rescued a fair lady from a giant's gate.
The night was dark and dungy beneath my feet.
Why, that giant, he nearly struck me dead,
But with my sword I did cut off his head.
I have searched and searched the world all round
But a man to my equal has never been found.
Is there a man who will before me stand?
I'll cut him down with my iron hand.
Who art thou?

Turkish Champion

In comes I, the valiant soldier,
Slasher is my name.
With sword and buckler down my side
I hope to win this game.

If that be he that standest there
Who slew my master's son and heir,
And if he sprang from royal blood
I'll make it flow like Noah's flood,
I'll cut thee, I will slash thee, and after that,
I will send thee over to Turkey Land to be made mince pies of.

King George

What! Thou black Morocco dog,
Let me hear no more of that,
For if I draw my deadly weapons
I shall surely break thy head.

Turkish Champion

How canst thou break my head,
When my head is made of iron,
My body armed with steel?
My hands and feet and knucklebones
I challenge thee to feel.

King George

Aha! What sayest thou?

Turkish Champion

What I say, I mean.

King George

Oh actor, actor, don't thee get too hot,
Thou dost not know whom thou hast got,
Pull off thy gloves and shield,
Take up thy sword and spear.
I'll fight thee without dread or fear.
Prepare! For life or death I do not care.

They fight, and Turkish Champion is slain.

Old Woman

Oh! King George, King George, what hast thou done!

Thou hast killed and slain my only son,

My only son, my only heir.

See how he lies bleeding there.

King George

He challenged me to fight with him;

And how could I deny?

In this battle either he or I must die.

Old Woman

Oh, a doctor, a doctor! Ten pounds for a doctor!

Is there ne'er a man to be found

To cure this man of his deadly wound?

Doctor Brown

Oyez! Oyez! In comes I, John Brown,

The best quick quack doctor in the town!

I am come to cure this man King George has slain.

Old Woman

How comes thou to be a doctor?

Doctor Brown

By my travels.

Old Woman

How far hast thou traveled, Doctor?

Doctor Brown

Through Italy, Sicily, France, and high Spain,

And now am returned to old England again

To cure all sorts of diseases.

Old Woman

What diseases canst thou cure?

Doctor Brown

The hipsy-pipsy, the palsy, the gout,

A man having twenty-two senses in his head,

I can cast twenty-one out.

Why I cured a snag tail last week nearly twenty-five feet long!

Surely I can cure thy son who is not quite gone.

Old Woman

What is thy charge, Doctor?

Doctor Brown

Five pounds, Martha.

Thee being an honest woman, I'll charge thee ten.

Old Woman

Cure him!

Doctor Brown

Here, man, take a drop of this nip-nap

Down thy tip-tap;

Take three drops out of this bottle.

Let it run down thy throttle!

Rise up, man, and fight the battle.

Turkish Champion does not rise.

Old Woman

Why, sir, thou art as green as grass.

Doctor Brown

Oh! Martha, I had quite forgot!

I pulled the wrong bottle off the wrong cork.

I have in my inside, outside, round-about backside waistcoat pocket

A bottle which my grandfather gave me,

Called ekee-okee adama pokee,

To bring any dead man back to life again.

Old Woman

Cure him!

The Doctor gives Turkish Champion a dose.

Turkish Champion

Oh! My back!

Old Woman

What ails thy back, my son?

Turkish Champion

My back is wounded, my heart is confounded,

Knocked out of seven senses into four-score,

Which was never known in England before.

Fool

So now we conclude and finish we must,

Put your hand in your pocket and pull your purse,

Put your hand in your pocket and see if all's right.

If you give naught, we take naught.

Farewell and good night.

All collect donations from the audience and exit singing a souling song—see page 181.

The Barley Mow

Now a popular drinking song, "The Barley Mow" used to be sung at harvest suppers throughout southern England. All who had helped with the harvest were invited to partake of roast beef, plum pudding, apple pie, and large quantities of ale or cider. According to an old Cornish account, the song accompanied the ceremony of replacing the previous year's "Neck" with the new one.

The Neck is another term for the "Last Sheaf" of corn or barley cut at the harvest. It was decorated with ribbons and carefully preserved inside the home to encourage a good harvest next year. In ancient times, it was believed that the Last Sheaf embodied the Corn Spirit, and that the man who cut it killed her. Consequently, it was considered very unlucky to be the cutter of the Last Sheaf. Sometimes the reapers stood around it and threw their sickles at it, thereby making the responsibility for the death more communal, much like the beheading in the longsword dance and Sword Dance Play.

But if one man's sickle obviously gave the last stroke, he was due some special treatment that varied from region to region. Sometimes he was given a small amount of money or certain privileges. However, in older times he was wrapped in the stalks he had just cut and jostled or handled roughly by his fellow harvesters. Like many other traditions with ancient roots, this was considered to be in jest or play by the time it died out, but it originally had a much more serious meaning. According to legend, the unfortunate cutter was sometimes sacrificed right there on the field to restore life to the Corn Spirit he had just killed.

* Each succeeding verse is added here.

1. Now here's good luck to the jill-pot,
   Good luck to the barley mow.
   Jolly good luck to the jill-pot,
   Good luck to the barley mow.
   The jill-pot, half-a-jill, quarter-jill,
   Nipperkin and the brown bowl.
   And here's good luck, good luck,
   Good luck to the barley mow.

2. Now here's good luck to the half-pint,
   Good luck to the barley mow.
   Jolly good luck to the half-pint,
   Good luck to the barley mow.
   The *half-pint, jill-pot, half-a-jill, quarter-jill,
   Nipperkin and the brown bowl.
   And here's good luck, good luck,
   Good luck to the barley mow.

3. Pint-pot

4. Quart-pot

5. Half-gallon

6. Gallon

7. Half-barrel

8. Barrel

9. Landlord

10. Landlady

11. Daughter

12. Slavey

13. Drayer

14. Brewer

15. Company

John Barleycorn

This drinking song tells of the birth, growth, and death cycle of the Vegetation God, depicted here as barley. True to legend, Barleycorn does not actually die but is magically reborn as a batch of fine ale!

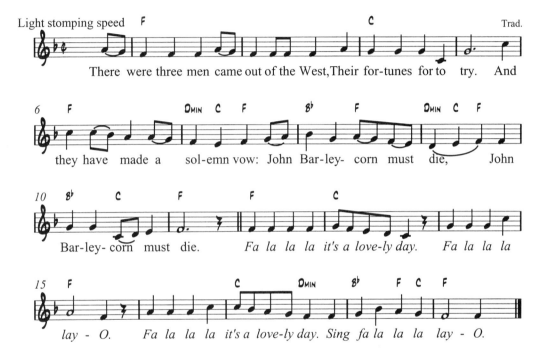

1. There were three men came out of the West,
   Their fortunes for to try.
   And they have made a solemn vow:
   John Barleycorn must die,
   John Barleycorn must die.

   Chorus:
   Fa la la la, it's a lovely day.
   Fa la la la lay-O.
   Fa la la la, it's a lovely day.
   Sing fa la la la lay-O.

2. They plowed him in three furrows deep,
   Lay clods all on his head.
   And they have made a solemn vow:
   John Barleycorn was dead,
   John Barleycorn was dead.

   Chorus

3. Well, then there came a shower of rain
   Which from the clouds did fall.
   John Barleycorn sprang up again,
   And he did amaze them all,
   He did amaze them all.

   Chorus

4. They let him stand 'til Midsummer's Eve,
   When he looked both pale and wan.
   And little Sir John's grown a long, long beard,
   And so became a man,
   And so became a man.

   Chorus

5. Well, then came men with great sharp scythes
   To cut him off at the knee.
   They bashed his head against a stone
   And they used him barbarously,
   They used him barbarously.

   Chorus

6. Well, then came men with great long flails
   To cut him skin from bone.
   And they even used him worse than that,
   They ground him between two stones,
   They ground him between two stones.

   Chorus

7. They wheeled him here, they wheeled him there,
   Wheeled him into a barn.
   And they have used him worse than that,
   They bunged him in a vat,
   They bunged him in a vat.

   Chorus

8. They worked their will upon John Barleycorn,
   But he lives to tell the tale.
   We pour him into an old brown jug
   And we call him home brewed ale,
   We call him home brewed ale.

The Keeper

Like the Abbots Bromley Horn Dance that mimics it, deer hunting most often takes place during the autumn months, at least on this side of the Atlantic. It would be very useful, then, to perform hunt magic in the form of music and dance during that time. However, unlike the Horn Dance, this song is not about deer hunting, but hints at activity more appropriate for, say, Beltane . . .

1. The keeper did a-shooting go,
    And under his coat he carried a bow,
    All for to shoot at a merry little doe
    Among the leaves so green-O.

    Chorus:
    Group 1: Jackie Boy?
    Group 2: Master?
    Group 1: Sing ye well?
    Group 2: Very well!
    Group 1: Hey down,
    Group 2: Ho down,
      All: Derry, derry down,
       Among the leaves so green-O.
    Group 1: To my hey down, down.
    Group 2: To my ho down, down.
    Group 1: Hey down,
    Group 2: Ho down,
      All: Derry, derry down,
       Among the leaves so green-O.

2. The first doe he shot at he missed.
    The second doe he trimmed, he kissed.
    The third doe went where nobody whist,
    Among the leaves so green-O.

    Chorus

3. The fourth doe she went over the brook.
    The keeper fetched her back with his crook.
    Where she is now you may go and look,
    Among the leaves so green-O.

    Chorus

4. The fifth doe she leapt over the plain.
   The keeper fetched her back again.
   Where she is now she may remain
   Among the leaves so green-O.

Chorus

5. Oh, the keeper did a-hunting go,
   And with his Earl he caught a doe.
   But she looked so sad that he had to let her go
   Among the leaves so green-O.

Chorus

A-Souling

Centuries before American children started soliciting candy door to door on the night of October 31, children in England begged passersby on the streets for pennies or soul-cakes. The pennies were used to buy masses for departed souls, the cakes to feed the souls when they passed by their old home. This tradition evolved from the earlier custom of a Dumb Supper or Feast of the Dead celebrated at Samhain. Families gathered to share a meal with those who had already crossed over, reserving an empty place at the table—complete with food, utensils, and drink—for unseen but much loved guests. Many contemporary Pagans, myself and my family included, celebrate a Dumb Supper every October 31.

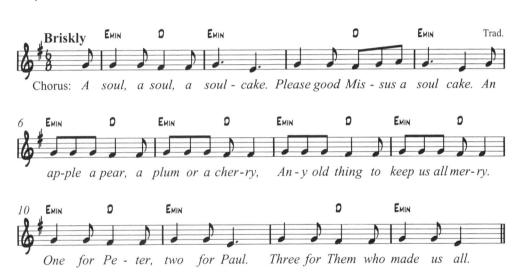

Chorus: *A soul, a soul, a soul-cake. Please good Mis-sus a soul cake. An ap-ple a pear, a plum or a cher-ry, An-y old thing to keep us all mer-ry. One for Pe-ter, two for Paul. Three for Them who made us all.*

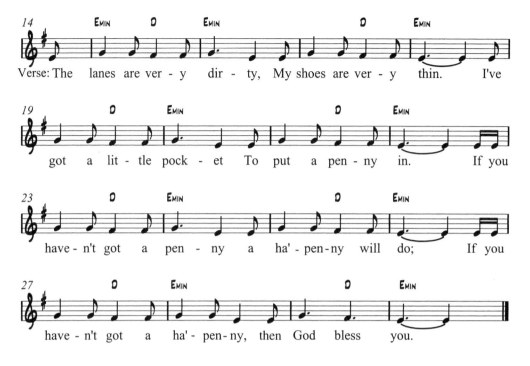

Verse: The lanes are ver - y dir - ty, My shoes are ver - y thin. I've got a lit - tle pock - et To put a pen - ny in. If you have - n't got a pen - ny a ha' - pen - ny will do; If you have - n't got a ha' - pen - ny, then God bless you.

Chorus:

> A soul, a soul, a soul-cake.
> Please good Missus, a soul-cake.
> An apple, a pear, a plum or a cherry,
> Any old thing to keep us all merry.
> One for Peter, two for Paul,
> Three for Them who made us all.

1. The lanes are very dirty,
   My shoes are very thin.
   I've got a little pocket
   To put a penny in.
   If you haven't got a penny,
   A ha'penny will do.
   If you haven't got a ha'penny
   Then God bless you.

   Chorus

2. God bless the master of this house,
   The mis-ter-ess also,
   And all the little children
   That 'round your table grow.
   Likewise young men and maidens,
   Your cattle and your store.
   And all that dwells within your house,
   We wish you ten times more.

   Chorus

Hop Tu Naa

As recently as the mid-1950s, children carrying carved turnip lanterns—similar to our jack-o'-lanterns—sang this song on the Isle of Man on Bonfire Night, November 5. Turnips, it should be noted, are much harder to hollow out and carve designs into than pumpkins. The experience is much like carving out a raw potato.

In older times, the proper date for this custom was November 11, which would have been October 31 before England adopted the Gregorian calendar in September, 1752. It was the beginning of the New Year and was called Hollantide or "Laa Houney" in Manx Gaelic.

1. 'Tis old Hollantide, *hop-tu-naa.*
   The moon shines bright, *trol-la-laa.*
   Hop-tu-naa as trol-la-laa.
   'Tis old Hollantide, *hop-tu-naa.*

2. Cock and hen, *hop-tu-naa.*
   Sup of the heifer, *trol-la-laa.*
   Hop-tu-naa as trol-la-laa.
   Cock and hen, *hop-tu-naa.*

3. What heifer shall we take?
   The little spotted one.

4. Quarter in the pot,
   I tasted the broth.

5. I scalded my throat.
   I ran to the well.

6. I drank my fill.
   Then coming back

7. I met a pole-cat.
   He grinned at me.

8. I ran to Scotland.
   What news was there?

9. The plough was ploughin',
   The harrows harrowin'.

10. A girl was cutting cheese.
    The knife was sharp.

11. She cut off her finger.
    She wrapped it in a cloth.

12. Locked it in a chest,
    It made stock and store.

13. Three brown sheep, *hop-tu-naa.*
    Had Will, the grandson, *trol-la-laa.*
    Hop-tu-naa as trol-la-laa.
    Three brown sheep, *hop-tu-naa.*

    (spoken)
    > If you give me anything,
    > Give it me soon.
    > For I want to go home
    > With the light of the moon.
    > *Hop-tu-naa.*

SONGS MAGICAL
BUT NOT SEASONAL

EVEN WHEN THEY DO NOT illustrate a particular season's customs or ceremonies, many traditional English folk songs have retained some essence of the old Pagan ways. The songs included here are only a small sample.

Thomas the Rhymer

A mortal's journey into Elfland, or the Otherworld, begins with a meeting between the mortal and a Guardian of the Otherworld: this is a common story in English folk balladry. The lyrics here refer to the tree whose fruit Thomas is forbidden to eat. Maybe the tree in question is the World Tree, the Tree of Life. Or perhaps eating the fruit would force him to stay in the Elf Kingdom forever—shades of the Persephone myth. The river of blood and the sound of the sea represent the primordial birthplace of all life. The fact that Thomas cannot see the sun or the moon indicates that he is truly in the Underworld.

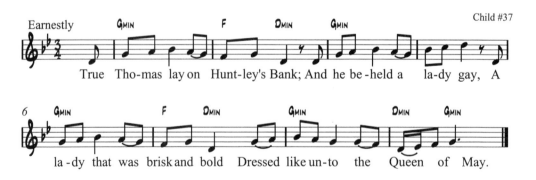

True Thomas lay on Huntley's Bank; And he beheld a lady gay, A lady that was brisk and bold Dressed like unto the Queen of May.

1. True Thomas lay on Huntley's Bank;
   And he beheld a lady gay,
   A lady that was brisk and bold
   Dressed like unto the Queen of May.

2. Her skirt was of the grass-green silk,
   Her mantle of the velvet fine.
   At each strand of her horse's mane
   Hung fifty silver bells and nine.

3. True Thomas he pulled off his hat,
   And bowed him low down on his knee.
   "All hail thou, mighty Queen of Heaven!
   For thy peer on Earth I never did see."

4. "Oh no, oh no, True Thomas," says she,
   "That name does not belong to me.
   I am but the Queen of fair Elfland,
   And I'm come here for to visit thee.

5. "But you must go with me now, Thomas.
   True Thomas, you must go with me.
   For you must serve me seven years,
   Through weal or woe as chance may be."

6. She turned about her milk-white steed,
   And took True Thomas up behind,
   And oh, whenever her bridle rang,
   The steed flew swifter than the wind.

7. For forty days and forty nights
   They rode through red blood to the knee,
   And he saw neither sun nor moon,
   But heard the roaring of the sea.

8. Oh they rode on, and further on,
   Until they came to a garden tree.
   "Light down, light down, you lady free,
   Some of that fruit let me pull to thee."

9. "Oh no, oh no, True Thomas," says she,
   "That fruit may not be touched by thee,
   For all the plagues that are in hell
   Light on the fruit of this country.

10. "But I have a loaf here in my lap,
    Likewise a bottle of claret wine.
    And now ere we go farther on,
    We'll rest a while, and you may dine."

11. When he had eaten and drunk his fill,
    "Lay down your head upon my knee,"
    The lady said, "ere we climb yon hill,
    And I will show you wonders three.

12. "Oh see you not yon narrow road
    So thick beset with thorns and briars?
    That is the path of righteousness
    Though after it but few enquires.

13. "And see you not that little braid road
    That lies across yon lily leven?
    That is the path of wickedness,
    Though some call it the road to heaven.

14. "And see you not that bonny road,
    Which winds about the fernie brae?
    That is the road to fair Elfland,
    Where you and I this night must go.

15. "But Thomas, you must hold your tongue
    Whatever you may hear or see.
    For if you speak in Elven land
    You'll never see your own country."

16. Soon they came to a garden green.
    She pulled an apple from a tree.
    "Take this for thy wages, True Thomas
    It will give thee tongue that can never lie."

17. "My tongue's my own," True Thomas said,
    "A goodly gift you would give to me!
    I neither care to buy or sell
    At fair or tryst where I may be.

18. "I will neither speak to prince or peer
    Nor ask of grace from fair lady."
    "Now hold thy peace!" the lady said,
    "For as I say, so must it be."

19. He has gotten a coat of the elven cloth
    A pair of shoes of velvet green.
    And 'til seven years were gone and past
    True Thomas on Earth was never seen.

Tom of Bedlam

A more proper title for this song is "Mad Maudlin's Search for Her Tom of Bedlam." Bedlam was the slang name for London's Hospital of St. Mary of Bethlehem, an asylum for male mental patients that opened around the year 1403. The corresponding institution for women was named for Mary Magdalene, shortened to Maudlin. The song depicts the quest of a woman driven mad by the loss of her lover, who is also mad.

This song is not considered "traditional" by folk music scholars. It was not among those collected from rural areas around the turn of the twentieth century, when most folk songs were written down. But lyrics about the antics of London's mentally ill were extremely popular in the 1500s and 1600s, and the text of this song, with a different tune, was published in 1720 by Thomas D. Urfey in *Pills to Purge Melancholy*.

A mere handful of centuries before then, the insane had been considered sacred, holy, able to walk in our world and the Otherworld at the same time. This may be the origin of the sacred Fool. How quickly Western society changed its opinion of such persons—from blessed messengers to people who needed to be locked up.

For to see mad Tom of Bed-lam, Ten thous and miles I'll trav-el. Mad
Maud-lin goes on dir-ty toes For to save her shoes from grav-el *Still I*
sing bon-ny boys, bon-ny mad boys, Bed-lam boys are bon-ny. *For they*
all go bare and they live by the air, And they want no drink nor mon-ey.

1. For to see mad Tom of Bedlam,
   Ten thousand miles I'll travel.
   Mad Maudlin goes on dirty toes
   For to save her shoes from gravel.

   Chorus:
   > Still I sing bonny boys,
   > Bonny mad boys,
   > Bedlam boys are bonny.
   > For they all go bare
   > And they live by the air,
   > And they want no drink or money.

2. I went down to Pluto's Kitchen
   For to beg some food one morning.
   And there I got souls piping hot
   All on the spit a-turning.

   Chorus

3. There I took up a cauldron
   Where boiled ten thousand harlots
   Though full of flame I drank the same
   To the health of all such varlets.

   Chorus

4. My staff has murdered giants,
   My bag a long knife carries
   For to cut mince pies from children's thighs
   With which to feed the fairies.

   Chorus

5. The spirits white as lightning
   Would on my journeys guide me.
   The moon would shake and the stars would quake
   Whenever they espied me.

   Chorus

6. And when that I'll be murdering
    The man in the moon to a powder,
    His staff I'll break and his dog I'll shake
    And there'll howl no demon louder.

    Chorus

7. By a knight of ghosts and shadows
    I summoned am to tourney.
    Ten leagues beyond the wild world's end;
    Methinks it is no journey.

    Chorus

8. Of forty bare years have I
    Twice twenty been enrage-ed.
    And of thirty been three times fifteen
    In durance soundly cag-ed.

    Chorus

9. With a host of furious fancies
    Of which I am commander,
    With a flaming spear and a horse of air
    Through the wilderness I'll wander.

    Chorus

10. I know more than Apollo,
    For oft, when he lies sleeping
    I see the stars at bloody wars
    In the wounded welkin weeping.

    Chorus

11. From the hag and hungry goblin
    That into rags would rend ye,
    May the spirit that stands by the naked man
    In the Book of Moons defend ye.

    Chorus

12. That of your five senses
    May you never be forsaken,
    Nor wander from yourselves with Tom
    Abroad to beg your bacon.

    Chorus

13. So drink to Tom of Bedlam,
    Go fill the seas in barrels.
    I'll drink it all well-brewed with gall,
    And Maudlin drunk I'll quarrel.

    Chorus

The Two Brothers

Myths of many cultures tell of the Dark Brother and the Light, eternally battling for the affections of the Lady: Robin Hood and the Sheriff of Nottingham, Horus and Set, Beli and Bran, to name a few. This is also the story of the Sacred King and his successor; one must die, and the other must take his place. At its most basic, the story brings us symbols of opposites—life and death, Summer and Winter, day and night—opposites that make the world what it is.

Traces of this song's Pagan roots can still be seen. The phrase "beneath a struggling moon" hints at a specific ritually significant time for the battle. In most versions of the song, the brothers engage in a wrestling match that turns into an accidental stabbing. The blood of the sacred victim, naturally, had to be spilled on the ground for the sacrifice to be successful. And again, if the killing was accidental, by "the hand of the Gods," the killer could not be brought to justice: another example of the ritual denial we saw in the mummer's plays. The young lady who revives the dead brother with her magical powers is, of course, the Goddess who brings her lover back to life every year.

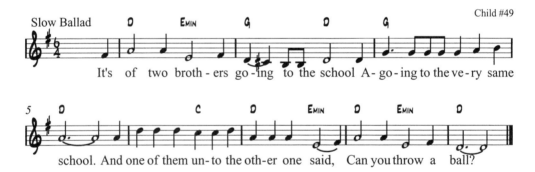

1. It's of two brothers going to school
   A-going to the very same school.
   And one of them unto the other said,
   "Can you throw a ball?"

2. "Oh, I can neither throw a stone,
   Nor can I throw a ball.
   But if you go down to the merry greenwoods,
   I'll throw you a wrestling fall."

3. Oh, they went down to the merry greenwoods
   Beneath a struggling moon.
   And a penknife fell from out John's pocket
   And gave him his dead wound.

4. "What will you tell my mother dear,
   This night when you come home?"
   "I'll tell her that you've gone to the western woods
   A-learning the hounds to run."

5. "What will you tell my father dear,
   This night when you come home?"
   "I'll tell him that you've gone to the foreign school,
   Your letters for to learn."

6. "What will you tell my true love dear,
   This night when you come home?"
   "I'll tell her that you're dead and in your grave,
   Where the small birds weep and mourn."

7. But when young Suzy heard of this,
   She charmed the birds from out their nests.
   She charmed young John out of his grave
   Where he was all at rest.

Willie's Lady

Aside from showing that conflict has always existed within witch families—related by blood or not—this song has some very useful anti-miscarriage spells in it. I have known witches whose pregnant coveners were in danger of giving birth too soon; they tied the "nine witching knots" in a cord, and the premature contractions stopped. Although this is not guaranteed to work, like most healing magic, it couldn't hurt.

When Francis Child published his paragon of cross-referencing, *The English and Scottish Popular Ballads,* a comprehensive collection also known as the Child ballads, he did not publish all the tunes that went with the old words. Although tunes for most of those traditional ballads have since been found and reattached to the lyrics, sometimes a tune from another place and time works well too. Although the poetry of "Willie's Lady" is unchanged since Child collected it, the tune shown here is from a Breton song, "Son ar Chistr," in praise of hard cider—a modern matchup.

-A- Young Wil-lie he sailed o-ver the rag-ing foam He's wooed a witch-wife and he's brought her home. He's wooed her for her long and gold-en hair, But his moth-er fash-ioned a might-y care. That though with child the la-dy be, She'd car-ry him for long and man-y's the year. But the babe she would nev-er bear.

-B- And there she lies in her bow-er in pain. And Wil-lie mourns his la-dy all in vain, Aye Wil-lie mourns her all in vain.

Seven-line stanzas go with "A" music.
Three-line stanzas go with "B" music.

1. Young Willie he sailed over the raging foam,
   He's wooed a witch-wife and he's brought her home.
   He's wooed her for her long and golden hair,
   But his mother's fashioned a mighty care.[1]
   That though with child the lady be,
   She'd carry him for long and many's the year,
   But the babe she would never bear.

2. And there she lies in her bower in pain,
   And Willie mourns his lady all in vain,
   Aye, Willie mourns her all in vain.

3. So Willie's gone for his mother for to find,
   The vilest witch over woman-kind.
   Saying, "My lady has a magic cup
   With gold and silver set about.
   This goodly gift shall be your own
   If you will let my lady bear her son,
   If you will let her bear her son."

4. "Oh, the child she'll never live to see
   Nor in good health shall she ever be.
   And she will die, and slowly turn to clay,
   And you will wed with another maid."
   "Another maid I'll never wed.
   Another maid shall never share my bed.
   I'd rather die," young Willie said.

---

1 Mighty care: terrible curse.

5. And there she lies in her bower in pain,
   And Willie mourns his lady all in vain,
   Aye, Willie mourns her all in vain.

6. So Willie back to his wicked mother's run,
   And he's gone there as a begging son.
   Saying, "My lady has a noble steed
   The likes of which you ne'er did see.
   And all about this horse's mane
   Are hanging fifty silver bells and ten.
   Fifty silver bells and ten."

7. "This goodly gift shall be your own
   If you will let my lady bear her son,
   If you will let her bear her son."

8. "Oh, the child she'll never live to see
   Nor in good health shall she ever be.
   And she will die, and slowly turn to clay,
   And you will wed with another maid."
   "Another maid I'll never wed.
   Another maid shall never share my bed.
   I'd rather die," young Willie said.

9. And though she lies in her bower in pain,
   The lady's told her Willie of a plan
   That she might bear their baby son.

10. Says she, "You must go get you down to the marketplace
    And you will buy a loaf of wax.
    And you must shape it in the like of a suckling babe.
    And you must make two eyes of glass.
    Then ask your mother to a saining day.[2]
    And stand nearby, as close as you can be
    That you might hear what she do say."

---

2 Saining day: child-blessing day for infants, like a baptism or a Wiccaning.

11. So Willie he has gone to the marketplace
    And he has bought a loaf of wax.
    And he has shaped it in the like of a suckling babe
    And he has made two eyes of glass.
    He's asked his mother to a saining day
    And he's stood as close as he could be
    That he might hear what she did say.

12. And how she raged and how she screamed.
    She saw a babe where no babe should have been,
    She saw a babe where no babe had been.

13. "Oh who's untied the nine witching knots
    that I hid among that lady's locks?
    And who has taken seven combs so fair
    That I had placed among that lady's hair?
    And who has slain the master kid[3]
    That ran and slept beneath that lady's bed
    That ran and slept beneath her bed?

14. "And who's untied her own left shoe?
    And who's undone what no one could undo?
    Who's undone what none could do?"

15. So Willie's untied the nine witching knots
    that had been hid among that lady's locks.
    And Willie's taken seven combs so fair
    That had been placed among that lady's hair.
    And Willie's slain the master kid
    That ran and slept beneath his lady's bed
    That ran and slept beneath her bed.

---

3 Master kid: young goat.

16. And he's untied her own left shoe.
    And he's undone what no one could undo.
    He has undone what none could do.

17. And when undone these things were done
    His lady brought forth unto him a son.
    His lady's brought forth a bonny son.
    Dai, dai, dai . . . (*Repeat syllable to end of "A" music*)

King Henry

The ghost in this story is really the Goddess in her Crone aspect. Many myths tell of the old, wizened terror who has sexual union with a knight—or other worthy mortal man—and is rejuvenated into her Maiden self.

Let nev-er a man a - woo-ing wend That lack-eth thing-es three: A

store of gold, an op - en heart, And full of chari - i - ty.

1. Let never a man a-wooing wend
   That lacketh thing-es three:
   A store of gold, and open heart
   And full of charity.

2. And this was seen of King Henry
   Though he lay quite alone.
   For he's taken him to a haunted hall
   Seven miles from the town.

3. He's chased the deer now him before
   And a doe down by the den.
   'Til the fattest buck in all the flock
   King Henry he has slain.

4. His huntsmen followed him to the hall
   To make them burly cheer,
   When loud the wind was heard to sound
   And an earthquake rocked the floor.

5. And darkness covered the hall
   Where they sat at their meat,
   The gray dogs, growling, left their food
   And crept to Henry's feet.

6. And louder howled the rising wind
   And burst the fastened door.
   And in there came a grisly ghost
   Stamping on the floor.

7. Her head hit the roof tree of the house,
   Her middle you could not span.
   Each frightened huntsman fled the hall
   And left the King alone.

8. Her teeth were like the tether stakes,
   Her nose like club or mell.
   And nothing less she seemed to be
   Than a fiend that came from Hell.

9. "Some meat, some meat, you King Henry,
   Some meat you give to me.
   Go kill your horse, you King Henry
   And bring him here to me."

10. He's gone and slain his berry brown steed
    Though it made his heart full sore.
    For she's eaten up both skin and bones
    Left nothing but hide and hair.

11. "More meat, more meat, you King Henry
    More meat you give to me.
    Go kill your gray hound, King Henry
    And bring him here to me."

12. He's gone and slain his good gray hound
    Though it made his heart full sore.
    For she's eaten up both skin and bones
    Left nothing but hide and hair.

13. "More meat, more meat, you King Henry,
    More meat you give to me.
    Go kill your goshawks, King Henry,
    And bring them here to me."

14. He's gone and slain his gay goshawks
    Though it made his heart full sore.
    For she's eaten up both skin and bones
    Left nothing but feathers bare.

15. "Some drink, some drink now, King Henry,
    Some drink you give to me.
    Oh, you sew up your horse's hide
    And bring some drink to me."

16. And he's sewn up the bloody hide,
    And a pipe of wine put in.
    And she's drank it up all in one draught
    Left never a drop therein.

17. "A bed, a bed now, King Henry,
    A bed you make for me.
    Oh, you must pull the heather green
    And make it soft for me."

18. And pulled has he the heather green,
    And made for her a bed.
    And taken has he his gray mantle
    And o'er it he has spread.

19. "Take off your clothes now, King Henry,
    And lie down by my side.
    Now swear, now swear, you King Henry,
    To take me for your bride."

20. "Oh, God forbid," says King Henry,
    "That ever the like betide.
    That ever a fiend that comes from Hell
    Should stretch down by my side."

21. When the night was gone and the day was come,
    And the sun shone through the hall,
    The fairest lady that ever was seen
    Lay between him and the wall.

22. "I've met with many a gentle knight
    That gave me such a fill.
    But never before with a courteous knight
    That gave me all my will."

Polly Vaughn

Ballet fans will recognize this song's story as similar to the plot of *Swan Lake*. Every culture has a story of animal transformation, perhaps the most widely known being the werewolf and the metamorphosis of maidens into birds. The spirit of a slain person coming back to explain the death—and perhaps to finger the guilty party—is a common theme in old ballads.

1. Come all you young fellows that carry a gun,
   I'll have you come home by the light of the sun.
   For young Jimmy was a fowler, and a-fowling alone.
   When he shot his own true love in the ruse of a swan.

2. As Polly went walking, a rainstorm come on.
   She hid under the bushes, the shower for to shun.
   With her apron wrapped over her, he took her for a swan,
   And his gun did not miss and it was Polly his own.

3. Then home rushed young Jimmy with his dog and his gun.
   Crying, "Uncle, dear Uncle, have you heard what I've done?
   Oh cursed be that gunsmith that made my old gun,
   For I've shot my own true love in the ruse of a swan."

4. Then out rushed bold uncle with his locks hanging gray,
   Crying "Jimmy, dear Jimmy, don't you run away.
   Don't you leave your own country 'til your trial's come on,
   For they never will hang you for the shooting of a swan."

5. Now the funeral of Polly it was a brave sight.
   With four and twenty young men, and all dressed in white.
   They took her to the graveyard and they laid her in the clay,
   And they bid adieu to Polly, and all went away.

6. Now the girls of this country, they're all glad we know
   To see Polly Vaughn a-lying so low.
   You could gather them into a mountain, you could plant them in a row
   And her beauty would shine amongst them like a fountain of snow.

7. Well the trial it wore on and young Polly did appear,
   Crying, "Uncle, dear uncle, let Jimmy go clear.
   For my apron was bound around me and he took me for a swan,
   And my poor heart lay a-bleeding all on the green ground."

The Darby Ram

In some parts of England, the Hobby Horse is a familiar figure at ritual dance and drama performances. In Wales, the *Mari Lwyd* (gray mare) is seen on special occasions. In Padstow, the Old Oss reigns every Beltane morning. But in the Midlands, Old Tup, covered with sheepskin and bearing a set of ram's horns, accompanies some very familiar characters, including a Fool and an Old Man. (Some folklorists say that the Darby Ram is another form of the Horned God.) They go from house to house acting out this song and begging for money. The Old Man knocks on the door and says:

Here comes me and my old lass
Short of money, short of brass
Fill up your glass, give us a sup
We'll come in and show you the Derby Tup.

This song also has some not-suitable-for-children verses. Catch me at a festival sometime, and I'll sing them for you!

1. As I went up to Darby, upon a Market Day,
   I spied the biggest ram, sir, that ever was fed on hay.
   Hey ringle dangle, hey ringle day.
   It was the biggest ram, sir, that ever was fed on hay.

2. This ram he had a horn, sir, that reached up to the sky.
   The eagles built their nests there, you could hear the young ones cry.
   Hey ringle dangle, hey ringle day.
   The eagles built their nests there, you could hear the young ones cry.

3. The wool upon this ram's back, it reached up to the moon.
   A man climbed up in April, and didn't come down 'til June.
   Hey ringle dangle . . .[4]
   A man climbed up in April, and didn't come down 'til June.

4. This ram was fat behind, sir, this ram was fat before.
   And every time his hoof went down, it covered an acre or more.

5. This ram he had four legs, sir, that stood incredible wide.
   A coach and six could drive right through with room to spare each side.

6. This ram he had a belly, sir, and so I heard them say
   And every time he ate a meal, he swallowed a rick of hay.

7. This ram he had a tooth, sir, in the shape of a huntsman's horn
   And when they'd opened it up, sir, they'd a thousand bushel of corn.

8. The butcher that killed this ram, sir, was up to his thighs in blood
   And the boy who held the basin was washed away in the flood.

9. And all the men in Darby came begging for his tail.
   To ring St. George's passing bell from top of Darby jail.

10. And all the women of Darby came begging for his ears
    To make them leather aprons to last them forty years.

---

4 Sing "Hey ringle dangle, hey ringle day" and the second line of the given verse.

11. Then all the boys in Darby came begging for his eyes
    To kick around the streets, sir, 'cause they were football size.

12. The wool that came from his back, sir, it was both thick and thin.
    Took all the women of Darby the rest of their lives to spin.

13. Took all the dogs in Darby to cart away his bones.
    And all the horses in Darby to roll away his stones.

14. O the owner of this ram, sir, he must be very rich.
    And the one who's sung this song, sir, is a lying son of a bitch!

All Around My Hat

Here is another spell, this one hiding in the innocent guise of a love song. An acquaintance of mine placed willow branches around the crown of her hat and instantly became obsessed with her absent lover. I don't recommend anyone try this.

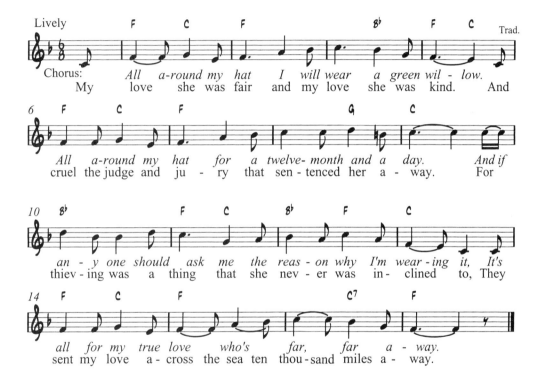

Chorus:

> All around my hat I will wear a green willow.
>
> All around my hat for a twelve-month and a day.
>
> And if anyone should ask me the reason why I'm wearing it,
>
> It's all for my true love who's far, far away.

1. My love she was fair and my love she was kind
   And cruel the judge and jury that sentenced her away.
   For thieving was a thing that she was never inclined to,
   They sent my love across the sea ten thousand miles away.

   Chorus

2. I bought my love a golden ring to wear upon her finger.
   A token of our true love and to remember me.
   And when she returns again we'll never more be parted.
   We'll marry and be happy forever and a day.

   Chorus

3. Seven, seven long years my love and I are parted.
   Seven, seven long years my love is bound to stay.
   Seven long years I'll love my love and never be false-hearted,
   And never sigh or sorry while she's far, far away.

   Chorus

4. Some young men there are who are preciously deceitful,
   A-coaxing of the fair young maids they mean to lead astray.
   As soon as they deceive them, so cruelly they leave them.
   I'll love my love forever though she's far, far away.

   Chorus

Lady Margaret and Sweet William

In the English folk ballad tradition, a symbolism code often explains the action. In this story, Lady Margaret dies, and her ghost, "all dressed in white," appears in the middle of the night to her false lover, William. The dream William has is also prophetic and symbolic. The blood indicates that his love has committed suicide. The visions of swine—animals of the Dark Goddess in her Crone aspect and underworld animals in their own right—confirm that Lady Margaret has indeed killed herself. Growing out of their graves, the rose, a sign of love, and the briar, symbolizing protection, indicate that their love has survived even though they did not.

1. Sweet William rose one May morning,
   And dressed himself in blue.
   Come tell to me about the love
   Betwixt Lady Margaret and you.

2. I know nothing of Lady Margaret
   And she knows nothing of me.
   But tomorrow morning by eight o'clock,
   Lady Margaret my bride shall see.

3. Lady Margaret was sitting in her high hall door.
   Combing her long yellow hair
   She saw Sweet William and his new-made bride
   Riding down the road so fair.

4. She threw down her ivory comb,
   Threw back her long yellow hair.
   Said, "I'll go down and bid them farewell
   And never more go there."

5. The day was past and the night had come,
   And they were all asleep.
   Lady Margaret appeared all dressed in white
   Standing at his bed feet.

6. "How do you like your snow-white pillow?
   And how do you like your sheet?
   And how do you like the fair young maid
   That lies in your arms asleep?"

7. "It's well I like my snow-white pillow,
   And well do I like my sheet.
   Much better do I like the fair young maid
   Standing at my bed feet."

8. The night was past and the day had come
   And they were all at work.
   Sweet William he was troubled sore
   By a dream he dreamed last night.

9. "Such dreams, such dreams they are no good.
   They are no good to me.
   I dreamed my hall was filled with swine
   And my true love stood in blood."

10. He rode 'til he came to Lady Margaret's hall
    And tingled on the ring.
    There was none so ready as Lady Margaret's brother
    To rise and let him in.

11. "Is Lady Margaret in the house,
    Or is she in the hall?"
    "Lady Margaret's lying in her cold black coffin
    With her face turned toward the wall."

12. "Fold back, fold back those snowy white robes
    Be they ever so fine.
    And let me kiss those clay cold lips
    For I know they'll never kiss mine."

13. Once he kissed her lily-white hand.
    And twice he kissed her cheek.
    Three times he kissed her clay cold lips
    And he died in her arms asleep.

14. Lady Margaret was buried in the old church yard.
    Sweet William buried beside her.
    And out her grave grew a red, red rose
    And out from his a briar.

15. They grew and they grew in the old church yard
    'Til they could grow no higher.
    And there they entwined in a true lovers' knot.
    The red rose 'round the briar.

The Wife of Usher's Well

Again, we need to translate the symbolism code to fully understand the magical elements of this song.

Journeys often indicate ventures into the Otherworld. In some versions of this song, the boys depart to learn their "grammerree" or grimoire—a book of magical arts. They die en route. Perhaps they were sacrificed. Perhaps their guides failed them and they were trapped in the Otherworld. Or perhaps they were initiated—initiation being a form of death and rebirth. Their mother, clearly a mage herself, forces their shades to return. They do so at Martinmas, which is very close to Samhain, when the veil between the world of the living and the world of the dead is thinnest. The boys are also wearing hats of bark, possibly from the World Tree, possibly of birch (birch has a long-standing connection to the dead). The hats keep them tied to the realm of the dead.

1. There lived a wife at Usher's Well
   And a wealthy wife was she.
   She had three stout and stalwart sons,
   And sent them o'er the sea.

2. They had not been away from home
   A week but barely one
   When word came to this carlen[5] wife
   That her three sons were gone.

_____

5 carlen: middle-class.

3. "I wish the winds may never cease
   Nor flashes in the flood.
   'Til my three sons return to me
   In earthly flesh and blood."

4. It fell about the Martinmas[6]
   The nights were long and dark.
   Three sons came home to Usher's Well
   Their hats were made of bark.

5. It neither grew in forest green
   Nor any wooded rise,
   But on the north side of the Tree
   That grows in Paradise.

6. "Blow up the fire my merry, merry maids
   Bring water from the well.
   For all my house shall feed this night
   Since my three sons are well."

7. Up then crowed the blood-red cock
   And up then crowed the grey.
   The oldest to the youngest said,
   "It's time we were away.

8. "For the cock does crow and the day does show
   And the channerin[7] worm doth chide.
   And we must go from Usher's Well
   To the gates of Paradise.

9. "Fare you well my mother dear,
   Farewell to barn and byre!
   And farewell to the bonny lass
   That makes my mother's fire."

---

6 Martinmas: on or about November 11.

7 channerin: muttering, mumbling.

The Two Magicians

This is the story of two powerful spellcasters with a difference of opinion about the nature of their personal relationship. Some sources cite this as a mythical combat between Merlin and Morgan Le Fay, others point to Gwion and Cerridwen's shapeshifting sequence in the Mabinogion. The song also notes the symbolism of the smith who is a mage as well. At one time, smithcraft was considered a mystical profession, and in several old accounts of witchcraft the village blacksmith was also the village High Priest.

1. Oh, she looked out of the window as white as any milk,
   And he looked in at the window as black as any silk.

   Chorus:
   > Hello, hello, hello, hello you coal black smith!
   > You have done me no harm.
   > But you never shall have me maidenhead
   > Which I have kept so long!
   > I'd rather die a maid, ah, but then she said,
   > And be buried all in my grave
   > Than to have such a
   > Nasty, husky, dusky, musty, fusty coal black smith.
   > A maiden I will die!

2. She became a duck, a duck all on the stream
   And he became a hunting dog and fetched her back again.

   Chorus

3. She became a star, a star all in the night
   And he became a thunder cloud and muffled her out of sight.

   Chorus

4. She became a ship, a ship out on the sea
   And he became a bold captain and boarded her did he.

   Chorus

5. She became a rose, a rose all in the wood
   And he became a bumblebee and kissed her where she stood.

   Chorus

6. She became a nun, a nun all dressed in white
   And he became a cantored priest and prayed for her by night.

   Chorus

7. She became a trout, a trout all in the brook
   And he became a feathered fly and fetched her with his hook.

   Chorus

8. She became a corpse, a corpse all in the ground
   And he became the cold clay and smothered her all around.

   Chorus

9. She became a quilt, a quilt upon a bed
   And he became a coverlet and took her maidenhead.

   Chorus

The Rattlin' Bog

This final song beautifully illustrates the circle of life and the connectedness of all beings. In this context, "rattlin'" means living or lively, not rattling or noisy.

Chorus:

Hi! Ho! The rattlin' bog and
The bog down in the valley-O.
Hi! Ho! The rattlin' bog and
The bog down in the valley-O.

1. In this bog there was a tree, a rare tree, a rattlin' tree. The tree in the bog and the bog down in the valley-O.

    Chorus

2. And on this tree there was a limb, a rare limb, a rattlin' limb. The limb on the tree and the tree in the bog and the bog down in the valley-O.

    Chorus

3. And in this limb there was a branch, a rare branch, a rattlin' branch. Branch on the limb and the limb on the tree . . . *[repeat the sequence]*

    Chorus

4. And on this branch there was a twig, a rare twig, a rattlin' twig. Twig on the branch . . .

    Chorus

5. And on this twig there was a nest, a rare nest, a rattlin' nest. Nest on the twig . . .

    Chorus

6. And in this nest there was a bird, a rare bird, a rattlin' bird. Bird in the nest . . .

    Chorus

7. And from this bird there came an egg, a rare egg, a rattlin' egg. Egg in the bird . . .

    Chorus

8. And in this egg there was a bird, a rare bird, a rattlin' bird. Bird in the egg . . .

    Chorus

9. And on this bird there was a feather, a rare feather, a rattlin' feather. Feather on the bird. . .

    Chorus

10. And from this feather there came a bed, a rare bed, a rattlin' bed. Bed from the feather . . .

    Chorus

11. And on this bed there was a man, a rare man, a rattlin' man. Man on the bed . . .

    Chorus

12. And with this man there was a maid, a rare maid, a rattlin' maid. Maid with the man . . .

    Chorus

13. And from this maid there came a child, a rare child, a rattlin' child. Child from the maid . . .

    Chorus

14. And on this child there was a hand, a rare hand, a rattlin' hand. Hand on the child . . .

    Chorus

15. And in this hand there was a seed, a rare seed, a rattlin' seed. Seed in the hand . . .

    Chorus

16. And in this seed there was a tree, a rare tree, a rattlin' tree. Tree in the seed . . .

CONCLUSION

Is the material in this book all there is to the English folk tradition?

Certainly not! These songs, dances, and plays represent less than ten percent of the material collected by folklorists in the last hundred years or so. The choice of these particular songs, dances, and plays was subjective, based solely on my own familiarity with them. Essentially, they are my favorites.

How, then, to best use the seasonal customs in this book to enhance your group or community's holiday celebrations? My best answer is to share my own experiences over the years. My group may not incorporate English folk traditions at every ritual, but here is how we have done so in the past:

- At Fall Equinox, we used the Abbots Bromley Horn Dance to cast the circle and mark sacred space.

- The focus of one Yule celebration was the St. George's mummer's play, and we have sworn Yule oaths holding the longsword lock.

- To illuminate our Samhain Dumb Supper, we carved turnips instead of pumpkins and dropped lit tea candles into them.

- One chilly Beltane, we added the Barber Pole and Gypsy Tent figures to our maypole dance, hoping to warm ourselves up!

- At the end of a community Lammas celebration, we sang "John Barleycorn" with everyone joining in on the chorus.

- The focus of one Summer Solstice ritual was the Robin Hood mummer's play.

The possibilities are endless.

A tradition can survive only if people still honor it and make it an important part of their lives. Although the traditions in this book are in no immediate danger of dying out, I encourage you to keep them, learn them, and pass them on to others.

And, above all, have fun with them!

APPENDIX A

Author's Note: If You Want to Learn More

If you are interested in learning more about the English and American folk traditions as they are practiced today, look into the Country Dance and Song Society of America, a national nonprofit membership organization.

Founded in 1915, the society is dedicated to preserving and promoting English and Anglo-American traditional and historical folk dance, music, and song. It maintains a comprehensive international list of groups: affiliate English country dance, American contra dance, morris and longsword, and folk-singing groups. The CDSS can help you find people in or near your town who get together and do these activities on a regular basis—sometimes weekly. I have never found a CDSS group that wasn't friendly to beginners. The society also has an extensive catalogue of books, recordings, and ritual dance supplies such as morris bells and longswords. Although the society is not particularly Pagan, I have found its members to be quite Pagan-friendly—as long as you keep your identifying jewelry to a discreet minimum.

Most important, through CDSS you can easily gain access to various week-long camps and weekend workshops where you can learn from the top dancers and singers in the country. These events sparked my passion for all things English-folkloric when, as a nine-year-old, I attended my first Christmas Country Dance School held in my own home-town of Berea, Kentucky.

If you don't happen to live near a large country dance community, the camps and workshops can also give you a chance to see some of the lesser-known aspects of the English folk tradition. As noted at the beginning of this book's Winter section, in 1998 I saw a mummer's play with a longsword dance that perfectly mimicked the sacrifice of the Sacred King. That performance took place at a folk festival the likes of which can be found in many parts of the country. At such festivals and camps I've also had the opportunity to watch the mysterious Abbots Bromley Horn Dance, see morris jigs that were new to me, and perform the Kirkby Malzeard longsword dance myself.

I hope to see you at a dance camp soon!

For more information, contact:

COUNTRY DANCE AND SONG SOCIETY OF AMERICA
132 Main Street
PO Box 338
Haydenville, MA 01039-0338
413-268-7426
www.cdss.org

APPENDIX B

Grounding and Centering

The folk dances and plays in this book, and possibly some of the songs, are capable of raising an incredible amount of energy when done with a proper ritual mindset. I learned this the hard way when I morris danced at a festival's opening ritual. The next thing I remember is waking up with ten people piled on top of me, trying to ground me and bring me back.

Therefore, I suggest that every participant ground and center before the activity begins, and thoroughly ground any excess energy afterwards. Below is one simple guide for grounding and centering; others may be substituted if the group so desires.

Before the Activity

Sit or lie down, whichever is more comfortable.

Begin by concentrating on your breathing. Inhale for a slow count of seven, hold your breath for a slow count of three, exhale for a slow count of seven, and hold for a slow count of three. Repeat.

On the next breath, push out your worries of the day as you exhale. On the next, try to relax your muscles as you exhale. Continue to breathe slowly and deeply.

Imagine that at the base of your spine is the taproot of a very large tree (you). Visualize slowly pushing that taproot down through whatever surface is directly under you. Push it farther down, through basement floors or whatever is below that, until you reach the Earth. Continue through all the layers of rock and soil until you reach the warm layer of energy at the Earth's center.

Slowly, with each deep inhale, pull that warm energy through your taproot, up past the rock and soil, past the surface you are sitting on, and into the base of your spine. It should feel warm and relaxing. As you inhale, flood your toes, feet, and ankles with this energy. They should be relaxed and centered. Inhale again, and fill your calves, knees, and thighs with the Earth's energy. Inhale again, and feel the energy relax your buttocks, hips, and lower abdomen. Once more and fill your ribs and diaphragm with warm energy. Take another deep breath and let your lungs expand with it. Another breath, and the energy flows out to your wrists, hands, and fingers. Inhale again, and relax your forearms, elbows, and upper arms. Take two or three breaths to fill your shoulders and neck with relaxing, warm heat. Inhale again, and feel your jaw, ears, and nose fill with the Earth's energy. Another breath, and relax your eyes, scalp, and forehead. One more breath, and let the energy fill the top of your skull, and begin to flow back down the outside of your body like a small shower. You should now be relaxed, connected to the Earth, focused, and ready to begin the activity.

Afterward

Sit or lie down on the floor or ground. Make sure your hands are resting with palms down on the surface. They are probably warm. Visualize all the excess energy you just raised pouring out of you and back into the Earth. Take your time. Be careful not to release too much energy and drain yourself; you want to keep what you would normally use. When you feel cooler and connected to the Earth again, you may get up.

APPENDIX C

Cleansing and Releasing Rite

Unfortunately, any horns you acquire for the Abbots Bromley Horn Dance probably come from an animal that died in a violent, painful manner. I recommend the antlers be ritually cleansed, and any lingering traces of the animal's soul released, before use. A ritual is included here as an example. Use as is or modify as needed.

Materials Needed

- Horns for cleansing

- Salt and water, mixed

- Sage leaves or smudge stick

- Tobacco, nuts, or small crystals (one pinch or item for each set of antlers)

Ritual Steps

Perform the ritual either alone or in a group, however you are most comfortable working.

1. Ground and center.

2. Prepare and cast the circle in the accustomed manner.

3. Invoke the four quarters in the accustomed manner.

4. Invoke the Goddess and the God in the accustomed manner. You may want to invite specific deities related to the forest, animals, or hunting, such as Diana or Artemis for the Goddess and Cernunnos, Silvanus, or Pan for the God.

5. Combine the salt and water, if you have not already done so. Three pinches of salt per bowl of water are sufficient. Take each set of antlers in turn and sprinkle liberally with the salt water, saying, "May healing water and cleansing earth wash away all pain."

6. Light the sage smudge stick or place the loose sage leaves on your incense charcoal, if you have not already done so. Take each set of antlers in turn and thoroughly cover with the smoke saying, "May fresh air and purifying fire burn away all pain."

7. Take each set of antlers in turn. If you know what animal they came from, you will name it: deer, elk, moose, for example. (Let's assume a deer.) Stand in the center of the circle holding the antlers aloft, and say, "I thank the spirit of this deer. Your gift is appreciated, and will be used with reverence and respect. So be it."

8. When all sets of antlers have been so handled, take the tobacco, nuts, or crystals in your hands and say, "No gift shall go unreciprocated. I offer these gifts in exchange for the antlers of my cousins, the deer. They shall be returned to the Earth as soon as I may."

9. Thank the Goddess and the God in the accustomed manner and dismiss.

10. Thank the Quarters in the accustomed manner and dismiss.

11. Dismiss the circle in the accustomed manner.

12. Ground any excess energy.

13. As soon as possible, take the gifts outside and give them to the Earth. Scatter the tobacco, leave the nuts for the squirrels, plant the crystals.

The rite is ended.

SELECTED BIBLIOGRAPHY

Alford, Violet. *Sword Dance and Drama*. London: Merlin Press, 1962.

———. *The Hobby Horse and Other Animal Masks*. London: Merlin Press, 1978.

Baskervill, Charles Read. "Mummers' Wooing Plays in England." *Modern Philology* XXI: 3 (1924): 225–72.

Billington, Sandra. *A Social History of the Fool*. New York: St. Martin's Press, 1984.

Brereton, Peter. *Through Britain on Country Roads*. London: Arthur Barker Ltd., 1982.

Brody, Alan. *The English Mummers and Their Plays: Traces of Ancient Mystery*. Philadelphia: University of Pennsylvania Press, 1969.

Bullen, Andrew. "The Abbots Bromley Horn Dance." *Country Dance and Song* (March 1987): 2–15.

Chambers, E.K. *The English Folk-Play*. Oxford: Oxford Clarendon Press, 1933.

Chappel, William. *Popular Music of the Olden Time*, Vol. II. London: Chappel & Co., 1855.

Chase, Richard. *Grandfather Tales*. Boston: Houghton Mifflin Company, 1948.

Davis, Michael Justin. *The England of William Shakespeare*. New York: Dutton, 1987.

Forbes, Rhomylly. *Links in a Thousand-Year-Old Chain: The Abbots Bromley Horn Dance in America*. Baldwin, KS: privately printed, 1997.

Frazer, Sir James George. *The Golden Bough: A Study in Magic and Religion*. New York: Macmillan Publishing Co., 1922. Reprint, New York: Collier Books, 1963.

Graves, Robert. *The White Goddess*. New York: Farrar, Straus & Giroux, 1948.

Hartley, Dorothy. *Lost Country Life*. New York: Pantheon Books, 1979.

Helm, Alex. *The English Mummer's Play*. Totowa, NJ: D.S. Brewer, Suffolk, and Rowman and Littlefield, 1981.

Hole, Christina. *A Dictionary of British Folk Customs*. London: Paladin Books, 1978.

———. *English Folk Heroes: From King Arthur to Thomas a Becket*. New York: Dorset Press, 1992.

Karpeles, Maud. *Cecil Sharp: His Life and Work*. Chicago: University of Chicago Press, 1967.

Kempe, William. *Nine Daies [sic] Wonder*. Ed. Edmund Goldsmid. Edinburgh: privately published, 1884.

Kennedy, Peter. *Folksongs of Britain and Ireland*. London: Oak Publications, 1975.

Morton, Thomas. *New English Canaan, Or New Canaan*. Amsterdam: 1637. Reprint Amsterdam: Theatrum Orbis Terrarum Ltd. and New York: Da Capo Press, 1969.

Myres, M.W. "Frodsham Soul-caking Play." *Folklore Journal* 43 (1932): 97–104.

Richards, Sandra. *The Rise of the English Actress*. New York: St. Martin's Press, 1993.

Ritchie, Jean. *Singing Family of the Cumberlands*. New York: Oxford University Press, 1955.

Rouse, W.H.D. "Staffordshire Folk and Their Lore." *Folklore Journal* 11 (1896).

Sharp, Cecil J. *English Folk Song: Some Conclusions*. London: Methuen & Co. Ltd., 1907.

———. *The Country Dance Book*. 6 vols. Surrey, England: Novello & Co., Ltd., 1909. Reprint, Leeds, England: Moxon Press, Ltd., 1985.

———. *The Sword Dances of Northern England*. London: English Folk Dance and Song Society, 1911. Reprint, 1985.

Sharp, Cecil J., ed. *One Hundred English Folksongs*. Boston: Oliver Ditson Company, 1916. Reprint, New York: Dover Publications, 1975.

Sharp, Cecil J. and Herbert C. MacIlwainy. *The Morris Book*. 5 vols. Yorkshire, England: EPS Publishing, Ltd., 1974–1975.

Stewart, Bob. *Where Is Saint George? Pagan Imagery in English Folksong*. Wiltshire, England: Moonraker Press, 1977.

Swahn, Jan-Ojvind: *Maypoles, Crayfish & Lucia: Swedish Holidays and Traditions*. Varnamo, Sweden: Falths, Tryckeri, 1994.

Tiddy, R.J.E. *The Mummer's Play*, Oxford: Clarendon Press, 1923. Reprint, Oxford, Norwood Editions, 1974.

Tierney, Patrick. *The Highest Altar*. New York: Viking Press, 1989.

Walker, Barbara. *The Woman's Encyclopedia of Myths and Secrets*. San Francisco: Harper & Row, 1983.

Wiles, David. *The Early Plays of Robin Hood*. Ipswich, England: D.S. Brewer, 1981.

Wolkstein, Diana and Samuel Noah Kramer. *Inanna, Queen of Heaven and Earth*. New York: Harper & Row, 1983.

Free Catalog

Get the latest information on our body, mind, and spirit products! To receive a **free** copy of Llewellyn's consumer catalog, *New Worlds of Mind & Spirit,* simply call 1-877-NEW-WRLD or visit our website at www.llewellyn.com and click on *New Worlds.*

LLEWELLYN ORDERING INFORMATION

Order Online:
Visit our website at www.llewellyn.com, select your books, and order them on our secure server.

Order by Phone:
- Call toll-free within the U.S. at 1-877-NEW-WRLD (1-877-639-9753). Call toll-free within Canada at 1-866-NEW-WRLD (1-866-639-9753)
- We accept VISA, MasterCard, and American Express

Order by Mail:
Send the full price of your order (MN residents add 6.5% sales tax) in U.S. funds, plus postage & handling to:

Llewellyn Worldwide
2143 Wooddale Drive, Dept. 978-0-7387-1500-1
Woodbury, MN 55125-2989

Postage & Handling:

Standard (U.S., Mexico, & Canada). If your order is:
$24.99 and under, add $3.00
$25.00 and over, FREE STANDARD SHIPPING

AK, HI, PR: $15.00 for one book plus $1.00 for each additional book.

International Orders (airmail only):
$16.00 for one book plus $3.00 for each additional book

Orders are processed within 2 business days.
Please allow for normal shipping time. Postage and handling rates subject to change.

Circle, Coven & Grove
A Year of Magickal Practice

Deborah Blake

Green, Celtic, Alexandrian, Eclectic . . . every circle, coven, and grove of Witches is as unique as the magick they practice. No matter what kind of Witch you are, High Priestess Deborah Blake's guide to group practice has something for you.

An instruction manual, workbook, and Book of Shadows all rolled into one, *Circle, Coven & Grove* is an ideal tool for busy Witches, new groups, new leaders, groups sharing leadership, and Wiccans seeking inspiration for crafting rituals. Blake provides original—yet easy to modify—group rituals for New Moons, Full Moons, and Sabbats for a full Wheel of the Year. There are seasonal spells, blessings, and rituals for celebrating holidays, increasing energy, giving thanks, healing, and more. Blake also discusses circle etiquette and the dos and don'ts of establishing a group or becoming a group leader.

978-0-7387-1033-4
264 pp., 7½ x 7½ $14.95

To order, call 1-877-NEW-WRLD
Prices subject to change without notice
Order at Llewellyn.com 24 hours a day, 7 days a week!

Natural Witchery
Intuitive, Personal & Practical Magick

Ellen Dugan

Natural Witchery offers dozens of ways to hone your intuition, enchance your magickal powers, and enliven your everyday practice.

Ellen Dugan goes to the heart of what it means to be a natural Witch. Forget about lineage, degrees, and politically correct titles. Her thoughtful observations and wise words will guide you back to what's important: forging your own unique spiritual path. These engaging exercises will help you look within yourself and stretch your psychic talents, discover your elemental strengths, and charge up your personal power.

Dugan's personal anecdotes and humor liven up the lessons and keep you grounded throughout the daily joys and trials of life as a natural Witch.

978-0-7387-0922-2
288 pp., 7½ x 7½ $16.95

Pagan Spirituality
A Guide to Personal Transformation

Joyce & River Higginbotham

In a world filled with beginner books, deeper explanations of the Pagan faith are rarely found. Picking up where their critically acclaimed first book *Paganism* left off, best-selling authors Joyce & River Higginbotham offer intermediate-level instruction with *Pagan Spirituality*.

Respected members of their communities, the Higginbothams describe how to continue spiritual evolution though magick, communing, energy work, divination, and conscious creation in a pleasant, encouraging tone. Learn how to use journaling, thought development, visualization, and goal-setting to develop magickal techniques and to further cultivate spiritual growth. This book serves to expand the reader's spiritual knowledge base by providing a balanced approach of well-established therapies, extensive personal experience, and question-and-answer sessions that directly involve the reader in their spiritual journey.

978-0-7387-0574-3
288 pp., 7½ x 9⅛

$14.95

Neopagan Rites

A Guide to Creating Public Rituals That Work

Isaac Bonewits

Isaac Bonewits pours over three decades of ritual experience—creating, attending, and leading cere-monies as a Neopagan priest and magician—into this practical guide to effective ritual. Ideal for Earth-centered spiritual movements and other liberal religious traditions, this book clarifies how to design powerful rites for small groups or large crowds.

Bonewits addresses every detail that contributes to successful public worship: the dynamics of participants, common worship patterns, the deities invoked, the risks of mixing spiritual traditions, pre-ritual preparation, and more. Learn to choose the optimal time, location, costume, props, and altar decorations. Enhance your ceremony with music, singing, poetry, dance, and movement. There are also invaluable tips for raising and channeling energy and using centers of power to send energy. Best of all, Neopagan Rites will help you create and perform rituals that unify, inspire, and fulfill their intended purpose.

978-0-7387-1199-7
240 pp., 6 x 9 $15.95

RitualCraft

Creating Rites for Transformation and Celebration

AMBER K & AZRAEL ARYNN K

From Sabbat events to magick ceremonies to handfastings, ritual is at the heart of Pagan worship and celebration. Whether you're planning a simple coven initiation or an elaborate outdoor event for hundreds, *RitualCraft* can help you create and conduct meaningful rituals.

Far from a recipe book of rote readings, this modern text explores rituals from many cultures and offers a step-by-step Neopagan framework for creating your own. The authors share their own ritual experiences—the best and the worst—illustrating the elements that contribute to successful ritual. *RitualCraft* covers all kinds of occasions: celebrations for families, a few people or large groups; rites of passage; Esbats and Sabbats; and personal transformation. Costumes, ethics, music, physical environment, ritual tools, safety, speech, and timing are all discussed in this all-inclusive guidebook to ritual.

978-1-56718-009-1

568 pp., 7 x 10 $24.95

To order, call 1-877-NEW-WRLD
Prices subject to change without notice
Order at Llewellyn.com 24 hours a day, 7 days a week!

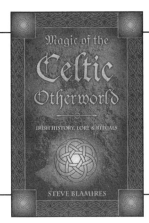

Magic of the Celtic Otherworld
Irish History, Lore & Rituals

Steve Blamires

Learn to live in harmony with the "Green World." Many people today distance themselves from the Earth. They forget they are a part of Nature. *Magic of the Celtic Otherworld* offers a holistic magical system that will break down the barriers between you and the natural world.

Drawing upon spiritual, Irish-Celtic tradition, history, and mythology, this book provides wondrous stories, seasonal rituals, and practical exercises that will expand your spiritual potential. This self-enriching journey to the mystical Otherworld will help you attune to Nature, channel magickal forces, and harmonize with the "Green World."

978-0-7387-0657-3
352 pp., 6 x 9 $16.95

A Year of Ritual

Sabbats & Esbats for Solitaries & Covens

SANDRA KYNES

It's easy to lose ourselves in the everyday business of life. One way to bring our bodies, minds, and spirits into alignment is through ritual celebrations. A vital part of Wicca and Paganism, ritual strengthens our connection to nature and helps us to enter the realm of the Divine.

For Witches and Pagans of all levels, *A Year of Ritual* provides ready-made rituals for a full year of Sabbats and Esbats. Groups or solitary participants can use these easy-to-follow rituals straight from the book. Ideas, words, and directions for each ritual are included along with background information, preparation requirements, and themes. This unique sourcebook also explains basic formats and components for creating your own rituals.

978-0-7387-0583-5
240 pp., 7½ x 9⅛ $14.95

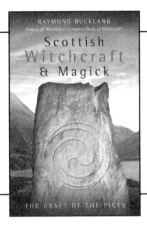

Scottish Witchcraft & Magick
The Craft of the Picts

Raymond Buckland

From the ancient misty Highlands of Scotland to modern-day America come the secrets of solitary Witchcraft practice. The author of *Buckland's Complete Book of Witchcraft* introduces "PectiWita," or the craft of the Picts. Learn the history of these mysterious early Keltic people, their origins, beliefs, and celebrations. This book also explores the magic, sacred tools, herbal lore, song and dance, and recipes of the Scottish PectiWita tradition.

978-0-7387-0850-8
256 pp., 5¼ x 8 $12.95

To Write to the Author

If you wish to contact the author or would like more information about this book, please write to the author in care of Llewellyn Worldwide and we will forward your request. Both the author and publisher appreciate hearing from you and learning of your enjoyment of this book and how it has helped you. Llewellyn Worldwide cannot guarantee that every letter written to the author can be answered, but all will be forwarded. Please write to:

Bronwen Forbes
℅ Llewellyn Worldwide
2143 Wooddale Drive, Dept. 978-0-7387-1500-1
Woodbury, MN 55125-2989, U.S.A.
Please enclose a self-addressed stamped envelope for reply,
or $1.00 to cover costs. If outside U.S.A., enclose
international postal reply coupon.

Many of Llewellyn's authors have websites with additional information and resources. For more information, please visit our website at:

www.llewellyn.com